"Finally, here is a work that offers heartfelt methods that move us beyond 'survivorhood' and helps us reclaim the soul of our lived experience. This book is brimming with intriguing and delightful exercises as Yvonne Dolan offers method after method to invite the reader to unlock and harness their inner resources, creating a renewed spirit of courage and hope and a map for getting the life they really want."
—Jim Duvall, Director, Brief Therapy Training Centres-International™ (*A division of C.M. Hincks Institute*)

"Yvonne Dolan's book, *One Small Step*, is an invitation to anyone with a dark history to come into their own with confidence and, even more, to explore and play with life and to be curious about all the richness and beauty available in ordinary magical lives. The exercises are enlivening and enlightening with a sensuality and connectedness to the world that is healthy and healing."
—Mary Kean, MA, RCC, editor of *Journal of Collaborative Therapies* and
   Arden Henley, MA, RCC, Director, White Rock Family Therapy Institute

"Reading this book, you will be touched by Yvonne's warmth, enabling you to take the first small step beyond being a survivor. Yvonne is a sensitive and thoughtful therapist, a good friend to many, and an internationally known lecturer and wise teacher."
—Insoo Kim Berg, coauthor of *Interviewing for Solutions*

"Dolan not only encourages readers to move beyond a survivor identity, she shows us how in small, easy-to-manage steps and exercises that will make a difference in every aspect of our lives. She writes beautifully and joins readers as a wise friend. Chock full of personal stories and practical suggestions, reading *One Small Step* may be the most important step a person could take."
—Jill Freedman, MSW, coauthor of *Narrative Therapy: The Social Construction of Preferred Realities*

Other books by Yvonne Dolan

*Resolving Sexual Abuse: Solution-Focused Therapy
and Ericksonian Hypnosis for Adult Survivors*

*A Path with a Heart: Ericksonian Utilization
with Resistant and Chronic Clients*

ONE
SMALL
STEP

Moving Beyond Trauma and Therapy
to a Life of Joy

YVONNE DOLAN, MA

Authors Choice Press
San Jose New York Lincoln Shanghai

One Small Step
Moving Beyond Trauma and Therapy to a Life of Joy

Authors Choice Press
an imprint of iUniverse.com, Inc.

For information address:
iUniverse.com, Inc.
620 North 48th Street, Suite 201
Lincoln, NE 68504-3467
www.iuniverse.com

Originally published by Papier Mache

ISBN: 0-595-12535-2

Printed in the United States of America

To my mother,
Barbara Ogle Dolan Taylor,
with love and gratitude for our long ago walks
in the woods in the rain and so much more

CONTENTS

A PERSONAL NOTE TO THE READER

Terrible things can happen in life with no warning, and afterward we have no choice but to carry on as best we can. I learned this at an early age. My first memory as a young child is of a memorial service for my father. There I witnessed firsthand the emotional devastation wreaked by war. My mother's and grandparents' hearts and spirits were broken when my young father was killed in the Korean War.

Very early on I grieved that my father was gone from the world before I even knew him. Despite my mother's love and her desire to shield me from harm, I suffered multiple episodes of sexual and emotional abuse during my childhood. At these times I tried to comfort myself by imagining that if my father had lived he would have protected me from the abusers.

As I grew to adulthood, I struggled to come to terms with these and other bad things that happened and to embrace the good in the world around me in order to find personal strength to make my life worth living.

Recorded between the lines of this book are my own journey and those of my psychotherapy clients, family, and friends who inspired me by their courage and determination to create lives that now shine brightly.

If you too have struggled with painful past events-or even if you have not—*One Small Step* will unlock psychological resources and abilities you may never have realized you had and empower you to create the life you want. I offer you this book as a talisman of hope and courage for your own journey. And even though I don't know you personally, I affirm my faith in your ability to create the rewarding life you've always deserved. I did it and believe me, you can do it too, beginning with one small step.

Wishing you all of life's blessings.

Yvonne Dolan

ONE
SMALL
STEP

Moving Beyond Trauma and Therapy
to a Life of Joy

MOVING BEYOND SURVIVORHOOD

*"If I had my life to live over, I would start barefoot earlier in the spring
and stay that way later in the fall. I'd go to more dances, I'd ride more
merry-go-rounds. I'd pick more daisies."*

—Nadine Stair, age eighty-five

"IT'S TIME TO GET ON WITH MY LIFE"

Maggie slumped on the couch in my office, fingers fidgeting in her jacket pocket, searching for the cigarettes she had given up several months ago. Her eyes were red from crying, and her voice trembled as she spoke.

> I've spent my whole life getting over what happened to me. I keep trying and trying to make a good life for myself, a happy life, but it never works out the way I hope. I've done all the things you're supposed to do to survive being abused as a kid, and to get over the other bad things that happened later. I'm thirty-two years old, and I'm tired of waiting. When am I going to start enjoying my life?

Maggie's awareness that she needs to move beyond surviving the past and start living a rewarding life, and her frustration at feeling stuck in her efforts to do so, reflect the experience of many people I have seen in my psychotherapy practice over the past twenty-three years.

The answer to Maggie's question is *now*. I wrote this book for people, like Maggie, who have endured traumas and now want to get on with living their lives. If you have survived pain—physical, sexual, or emotional abuse; divorce or relationship difficulties; financial problems; illness or accidents; loss; or other traumatic life experiences—and want to finally live with joy, this book is for you.

This book is especially intended for the person who is willing, but at times finds it difficult, to embrace the future with joy.

One Small Step is an invitation to create the kind of future that you want to live, regardless of what happened or was done to you in the past. If you are wondering whether this applies to you, ask yourself this question: "Why settle for anything less?"

Maggie is not just going to start living her own life, she is going to give herself a good life, a life that authentically reflects the self she was born to be and will restore her capacity to experience joy.

SMALL STEPS TO A REWARDING LIFE

Regardless of what happened in the past, you can begin to create a rewarding and satisfying life for yourself now. This book will guide you through the process of creating the life you've been wanting, one small step at a time. As you progress through the chapters, your hopes and dreams will gradually become far more vivid and compelling than past experiences, resulting in a restored sense of wonder and joy in living that you may have feared was gone forever. Approaching cherished hopes and dreams one step at a time makes them less daunting and, most important, makes them undeniably achievable in real everyday life.

WHY VIEWING YOURSELF AS A SURVIVOR IS NOT ENOUGH

I originally decided to write this book because I was troubled by the emergence of a "survivor culture" in America. In attempting to respond to the very real and pervasive phenomenon of victimization, the psychotherapy profession inadvertently created a Survivor Identity.

I do not believe this phenomenon has occurred as a result of the wrongness of past ideas about what helps people recover from abuse and other traumas. Rather, it has occurred because psychotherapists have not yet extended ideas about recovery far enough to help people move beyond Survivorhood. Overcoming the immediate effects of abuse, loss, or other trauma and viewing yourself as a Survivor rather than a Victim are helpful steps, but ultimately not sufficient to help people fully regain the ability to live a life that is more compelling, joyous, and fulfilling than the past.

While many self-help books have documented the painful effects of victimization and the value of recognizing oneself as a survivor, no one warned us about the negative consequences that can result from continuing to think of oneself primarily as a Survivor over an extended period of time.

Unfortunately the Survivor mind-set that people typically develop to get through painful past experiences can later interfere with their capacity to fully enjoy life. People who embrace "survivor" as their primary identity over the long-term tend by necessity to filter daily living experiences through two criteria: how a current event resembles or differs from the traumatic thing that happened in the past, and how a current experience mitigates or worsens the continuing effects of the past trauma.

As a result, people who remain at the Survivor stage see life through the window of their Survivorhood rather than enjoying the more immediate and unconstricted vision of the world around them that they were originally born with. Such a limited view diminishes your ability to experience, much less, enjoy the moment. This inability to truly appreciate your present life can also interfere with your capacity to fully enjoy a healthy rewarding sexual relationship with a partner.

The idea that continuing to think of oneself primarily as a Survivor over an extended period of time was not helpful first occurred to me in the late 1980s when numerous psychotherapists attending my seminars on treatment of sexual abuse and other trauma throughout the U.S. and Canada described a puzzling phenomenon.

Many of their patients who had described themselves as Survivors (of abuse) over an extended period of time seemed to be suffering from a low-grade depression and expressed pessimism about the possibility for happiness in the future. Furthermore, these patients complained that they found themselves constantly evaluating the present in comparison with the things they had survived in the past and had trouble enjoying themselves in the moment.

Later, in 1995, I noticed a phenomenon that suggested that moving beyond thinking of oneself as a survivor could be a valuable step. I had just begun interviewing people for a small pilot study exploring the characteristics of people who had suffered sexual abuse earlier in life and were now living healthy, satisfying lives characterized by enduring relationships, meaningful work, and an absence of debilitating psychiatric symptoms.

Of the twenty people I interviewed, not one of them used the words *victim* or *survivor* to describe how they currently viewed themselves. I was not surprised at the absence of Victim as a characterization, since by definition these were folks who had managed to get beyond their victimization when functioning in life. But I was puzzled by the absence of Survivor as a descriptor in their responses to questions about how they thought of themselves.

When I asked the various interviewees what they thought about Survivor as a label, there was a striking consistency in their responses. They told me, "Yes, I survived what happened to me, but that's not who I am now," or "That's not how I think of myself now." Or they answered, "I haven't thought about myself that way for a long time," or "Well, that's part of me, but that's not all of who I am," and other similar responses.

In contrast, many of the people seeking my help as a psychotherapist seemed to be experiencing the phenomenon described by the psychotherapists attending my seminars. Repeatedly these clients told me, "I'm a survivor of sexual abuse [or physical abuse, or emotional abuse, or other trauma], and I've done all the right things the books say we're supposed to do to get over it, but I'm still not happy."

These people were not lazy or what doctors sometimes call malingerers. They were genuinely and earnestly trying to get on with their lives. And like Maggie, they were frustrated as hell. It gradually dawned on me that in creating the label of Survivor, the psychotherapy field had created the potential for a new set of problems.

THE OLD STAGES AND THE NEW ONE

As a psychotherapist interning at a telephone crisis center in the 1970s, I was taught that there are two stages of recovery from traumas involving emotional, physical, or sexual abuse, and other disastrous life events. The Victim Stage is necessarily the beginning of healing. When you first face the reality of a bad thing that was done to you or the bad thing(s) that happened to you, you begin to acknowledge the feelings (usually grief and anger) that accompany this.

Allowing yourself to feel these emotions and express them is a vital part of the healing process and a valuable aspect of the Victim Stage. Furthermore, realizing that you have been victimized implies that you recognize that what happened was not your fault.

Recognizing that you have been a victim of circumstances or other people serves the important purpose of allowing you to let go of self-blame and shame. Another aspect of recognizing yourself as having been a victim is finding the courage to tell someone else what happened to you.

Telling your story to a compassionate listener breaks down the isolation that causes fear and shame. You are no longer alone with the bad thing that happened or was done to you. The disadvantages of the Victim Stage are those that occur if a person continues to identify with the Victim Identity beyond its usefulness.

Once you have identified and expressed the feelings that resulted from being victimized, broken down the isolation by telling a caring person what happened to you, and realized that you are not to blame for abuse or other bad things that were done to you, the Victim label has done its work.

Continuing to think of yourself primarily as a Victim beyond that point can eventually lead to feelings of helplessness, despair, and a resulting passivity that can make you vulnerable to further victimization. As soon as you realize that you are not to blame for the bad thing(s) that happened, it is time to recognize yourself as a Survivor.

The Survivor Stage begins when you understand that you have lived beyond the time at which the traumatic experience occurred. Thinking of yourself as a survivor has many advantages. "Survivor" undeniably reinforces the fact that the abuse or other traumatic event is in the past.

Realizing that you survived leads to wondering, "How did I manage it? How was I able to survive this?" Acknowledging that you are a Survivor invites you to develop an inventory of those positive personality characteristics that allowed you to survive what happened, to identify and appreciate the internal strengths (knowledge, courage, spirituality, or other positive aspects of yourself) and external resources (friends, supportive family members, community support) that you already possessed at the time of the trauma or developed afterward in order to survive it.

A significant hallmark of the Survivor Stage is your regained ability to function productively in everyday life. A Survivor is able to focus on daily activities such as work, child care, household duties, community activities, hobbies, and spending time with friends.

Once you recognize that you have lived past the occurrence of the traumatic event and you acknowledge and appreciate the strengths and resources that have allowed your survival and eventual well-being, the Survivor Identity has done its work. For people who permanently remain at this stage, life is constantly filtered through the window of their Survivorhood. All events are evaluated in terms of how they resemble, differ from, mitigate, or worsen the effects of past events. This diminishes their ability to fully experience and enjoy life and is, I believe, responsible for the flatness and low-grade depression reported by so many self-described survivors of sexual abuse and other painful life events.

As Clarissa Pinkola Estes explains in her wonderful book *Women Who Run with the Wolves*:

> *If we stay as survivors only, without moving to thriving, we limit ourselves*
> *and cut our energy to ourselves and our power in the world to less than half.*

Estes goes on to suggest that rather than becoming a permanent primary identity, Survivor needs to ultimately become "one of many badges" that you wear, a source of pride but not the determinant of your identity.

Survivor is not a part of yourself that should be discarded, but rather appreciated as a significant aspect of yourself. Embraced in this way, surviving the trauma you endured is an accomplishment you can continue to celebrate without suffering negative consequences. Furthermore, such an incorporation will allow you to move on and create the life you so richly deserve.

Recently, I have been heartened to hear psychotherapists and support group members echoing the need for people to move beyond thinking of oneself primarily as a Survivor. In some psychotherapy circles, this next phase has been referred to as a "thriver" stage. While vaguely defined up until now, the notion of a third stage indicates that people are beginning to realize that more is needed.

In thinking about this third stage, I have struggled with what to call it. Initially I liked the term *thriver* because of its positive connotation. But it rhymes with *survivor* which may have negative connotations for people who are trying to leave painful memories behind.

Then it dawned on me. In retrospect, it seems obvious: The third stage is the stage in which you fully, joyously, and authentically become yourself. You began living not only in reference to bad things you survived or even in reference to present experiences and hopes for the future, but according to the totality of who you really are as a person deep inside. You become your truest self completely and enjoy the rewards of doing so.

Your Authentic Self Identity allows you more freedom than either of the preceding roles. Thinking of yourself in this way will enable you to experience a more compelling present and contemplate a future more vivid and fulfilling than your past.

You will be able enjoy life to the fullest: exulting in experiences that reach the potential you were born with, expressing yourself in the most personally rewarding and creative ways available to you as you go through your daily life. Your current experiences and relationships will increasingly evoke a sense of immediacy, wonder, and enhanced potential for growth.

So what could be disadvantageous about identifying with your Authentic Self, embracing your potential to fully experience life and express all the gifts you were born with? While the drawbacks are minimal in comparison to the advantages, it is only fair to state them. When initially connecting or reconnecting with your Authentic Self, this new way of thinking may feel unfamiliar, and therefore uncomfortable.

Over time as you continue to live in harmony with your Authentic Self, your lifestyle, relationships, and life decisions may be less predictable and more complex than they were when you primarily identified with the Survivor or Victim images. From the vantage point of your Authentic Self, you should become increasingly secure with and trusting of your knowledge and abilities. Consequently you may become less invested in maintaining the status quo in your life, and therefore less willing to squander your time and energy on relationships or situations that have become abusive or toxic for you. Instead you will devote your time and energy to the life you truly want and deserve to live.

HOW TO USE THIS BOOK

This book can be used in several ways: as a series of mental exercises, or as a daily or weekly format for your personal journal. You can record your responses to the exercises on paper or on audiotape, or just think about your responses if you prefer.

No matter how you chronicle your responses, the most important result of continuing to take small steps toward becoming aligned with your Authentic Self will be the rewarding changes that allow you to confidently pursue your hopes and dreams.

This book is divided into four part. The first part, "Enjoying the Gifts of the Present," is dedicated to exploring and expressing your Authentic Self. Chapter One, "Getting to Know Your Authentic Self," is devoted to investigating, identifying, and appreciating who you really are deep inside, beyond whatever bad things happened to you in the past. Chapter Two, "Welcome Home!," invites you to develop new ways to express and enjoy yourself at home. Chapter Three, "Enjoying Yourself More at Work" offers ideas for making the work environment a place that enhances rather than detracts from your quality of life.

Part Two, "Creating a Joyous Future," invites you to reclaim cherished hopes and dreams, to begin to make them realities, and to create time to enjoy the results. Chapter Four, "Hopes and Dreams," guides you through identifying what you really want from your life now. Chapter Five, "Yes, You Can!," offers strategies for transforming seemingly impossible or daunting goals into realistic possibilities. Chapter Six, "Time on Your Hands," provides ideas for changing how time effects your ability to realize goals and enjoy your everyday life.

Part Three, "Responding to Life's Challenges," helps you identify what really works best for you when people, memories from the past, or demands of the present threaten the gains you've made in creating the life you deserve. Chapter Seven, "Partners, Parents, Kids, and Extended Family," provides guidelines to help you identify ways to be creative, flexible, and true to yourself while responding to the needs of the people you love. Chapter Eight, "Coping When the Past Rears Its Ugly Head," offers ways to limit or permanently resolve residual effects of posttraumatic stress in your life. Chapter Nine, "Dealing with Rainy Days and Dark Nights," provides sensible coping strategies for getting through the blues that are occasionally a byproduct of living a heartfelt life.

Part Four, "Support and Further Resources," helps you maintain the momentum you've built up as you've progressed through the earlier sections of the book by inviting you to connect with supportive, like-minded people in person or through literature. Chapter Ten, "How to Start a Small Steps Support Group," supplies the specifics you need to start and continue an ongoing group of people dedicated to supporting one another's exploration and positive expression of life beyond Survivorhood.

A Suggested Reading List offers a selection of books you may want to reference for further exploration. Finally, there are blank pages in which to record important thoughts and insights that occur to you as you continue to pursue and develop a good life for yourself.

ORIGINS OF THE TECHNIQUES IN THIS BOOK

One Small Step is not intended as a substitute for psychotherapy; however, the exercises throughout have been carefully designed according to psychotherapeutic principles in order to evoke feelings of comfort and reassurance and to empower the reader to identify, explore, and expand her own unique solutions to the "problem" of creating a joyous, healthy, and rewarding life in the future that extends beyond Survivorhood.

The exercises in this book are derived from principles and psychotherapy techniques of Solution-focused therapy (Berg, 1990; Berg and Miller, 1992; Berg, 1994; Berg and de Shazer, 1993; de Shazer, 1982, 1985, 1991, 1994; de Shazer, Berg, Lipchik, Nunally, Molnar, Gingerich, and Weiner-Davis, 1986; Dolan, 1989, 1991, 1994a, 1994b; Furman and Ahola, 1992; Furman and Ahola, 1994; Lipchik, 1988; Lipchik and de Shazer, 1986; O'Hanlon and Weiner-Davis, 1989; Weiner-Davis, de Shazer and Gingerich, 1987).

Basic to this approach is the concept of the client and therapist cocreating solutions (O'Hanlon and Weiner-Davis, 1989). This idea is based on the respectful assumption that psychotherapy clients merit highly individualized and uniquely effective solutions to the problems that bring them to therapy, and that these solutions can be elicited through therapists asking meaningful questions.

Solution-focused therapy assumes that constructing a solution is a joint process between client and therapist, with the therapist taking responsibility for empowering the client to create and experience her own uniquely meaningful and effective therapeutic changes. This posture of respect, pragmatism, and hopefulness is uniquely suited to people who have survived physical, emotional, and sexual abuse and other traumas.

While consistent with Solution-focused concepts, the Ericksonian Relaxation Method in Chapter One and the Symbol for the Time of Your Life centering technique in Chapter Six are derived in part from the psychotherapeutic principles of Ericksonian Utilization. Closely related to the Solution-focused approach, Ericksonian Utilization (Erickson, 1958, 1959, 1965; Erickson, Rossi and Rossi, 1976; Dolan, 1985) was developed by Milton Erickson, MD, a psychiatrist.

The Ericksonian Utilization approach is based on the principle that psychotherapy clients' already existing perceptions, life experiences, behaviors, and personality traits are potentially valuable resources that may be incorporated into the therapeutic change process to relieve symptoms and improve the client's quality of life.

The Utilization concept implies that every part of the person's behavior, personality traits, relationships, personal beliefs, and values is potentially valuable and useful in enabling them to achieve more rewarding choices and experiences in life. Based on this concept, the Ericksonian relaxation exercises I include in this book invite the client to utilize aspects of previous moments in everyday life in which she has felt comfortable, centered, and relaxed in order to reelicit these feelings when needed in the present.

My own work as a psychotherapist treating survivors of sexual abuse and other traumas using a Solution-focused therapy and Ericksonian approaches is documented in *Resolving Sexual Abuse: Solution-Focused and Ericksonian Hypnosis for Adult Survivors* and in various journal articles and book chapters. I have been training psychotherapists in Solution-focused techniques for ten years, and conduct seminars at universities, hospitals, and mental health centers throughout the U.S. and Canada, and in Europe, South America, Australia, and Asia.

AND NOW TO BEGIN

I am inviting you to make a commitment. Not to me, nor to this book, but to yourself. I suggest that you devote at least one hour a week to implementing the ideas described in this book. Certainly, you may decide to spend more time, but even an hour a week will yield results. Change is inevitable. Our goal here is to increase the percentage of changes that happen in your life that are to your liking, and to empower you to create the changes you desire through a series of inviting small steps that you'll want to do.

I realize that by the time you are reading these words, you may have been badly battered by life, and may be experiencing the cynicism and despair that sometimes result. Nevertheless, the meaning of these words applies to you. (I assure you, it does!) Step by step you will build or reclaim the life for which you secretly long, a life beyond the past that joyously and completely reflects who you really are.

PART ONE

Enjoying the Gifts of the Present

CHAPTER ONE

GETTING TO KNOW
YOUR AUTHENTIC SELF

When what we do grows out of inner conviction that
whatever it may be that we choose to do in a moment or in
our lifetime is meaningful, there is soul in the choice.

—Jean Shinoda Bolen

. . . I saw a strikingly handsome Japanese tea bowl that had been broken
and pieced together. The image of that bowl made a lasting impression. Instead
of trying to hide the flaws, the cracks were emphasized, filled with silver. The
bowl was even more precious after it had been mended.

—Sue Bender

Imagine that you have just found out you own a wonderful home on a beautiful estate. The house reflects your special and unique values and tastes, and the climate there is in beautiful harmony with your moods.

You have owned this wonderful acreage and the home on it all your life, since earliest childhood, but at some point you were forced to move away from it. It may have been a long while since you visited your lovely home and delighted in the beautiful grounds, trees, flowers, and other well-cared-for living things in the surrounding acreage.

You may have forgotten what your house and estate look like or even that you own them. Perhaps you were told long ago (wrongly!) that the house and its beautiful lands no longer belonged to you. Or maybe, early in childhood, you were given the message that you could no longer live there if you wanted to be loved by your parents or other caregivers. Regardless of any messages other people sent you, this estate always has belonged and always will belong to you and you alone. The estate and the wonderful home it surrounds is your Authentic Self.

It is now time to return and reacquaint yourself with your personal estate—your Authentic Self—so you can fully experience all of its rewards and delights. You'll know you are truly reunited with your Authentic Self when your life is infused with wonder and joy. Welcome home!

What is your Authentic Self? In times of emotional calm, it is your psychological sanctuary deep within, the place where you can heal your wounds, explore and embrace the deeper longings of your heart, and take delight in the experience of being alive.

In times of crisis or intense emotional experiences, your Authentic Self is an island of safety and constancy that remains solid and intact, like a lighthouse beckoning reassuringly beyond the ravages of winds and stormy seas. Your Authentic Self exists beyond the weather of your constantly changing emotions, thoughts, and opinions. It is:

> *That "you" (that is) the unchanging presence or permanent "I" that witnesses all of the changing "I's," i.e., I feel good, I feel bad, I like you, I don't like you. (Wolinsky, 1996)*

This chapter is organized into three sections designed to help you move into the estate of your Authentic Self. The first section will strengthen and replenish you as you explore your Authentic Self through words. The next section will assist you in creating a symbolic representation of your Authentic Self. The final section, which focuses on relaxation and play, will guide your exploration of your inner resources through a powerful self-relaxation technique and a "date" or mini-vacation with your Authentic Self.

If these activities initially strike you as frivolous or self-indulgent, remember that loving, exploring, and honoring the person you really are deep inside will further develop and enhance your capacity to love and nurture others as well as yourself. When you suffer an inability to love and appreciate yourself, you are equally unable to fully love another person.

EXPLORING YOUR AUTHENTIC SELF THROUGH WORDS

We are able to learn a surprising number of things about ourself through creative writing. The following will amaze and delight you with personal insights reenforcing your sense of value and reminding you of the special characteristics you bring into the world.

Keeping a Journal

I strongly encourage you to purchase a journal for yourself at this point. Having one place in which to record your thoughts, ideas, observations, and responses to the exercises in this book will support the importance of your work exploring your Authentic Self.

When choosing a journal, look for a size that is comfortable for you to carry with you and a page size that works well with the size and style of your handwriting. Choose a journal in a color or print that delights you. If you cannot find one that appeals to you, make a cover for your journal out of pretty fabric or wrapping paper. You can make your customized cover more durable by adding a second cover of clear adhesive-backed contact paper.

A journal is an ongoing gift that you give yourself. Daily entries ensure a continuing dialog with your Authentic Self. A journal notebook or ongoing tape recording is a friend that is always available to listen and always understands, even in the wee hours of the night.

If you find that you have little to say on some days, don't worry. This does not signify a lack of progress, but is a normal occurrence among journal writers. Feeling empty of your own words may mean you are ready to absorb more learning from other people.

Perhaps you have heard the proverbial story of the pilgrim who visits a famous teacher, hoping to learn from him. The teacher asks the pilgrim to pour him a cup of tea, instructing him, "I will tell you when to stop." To the pilgrim's horror, the teacher says nothing and the tea spills over the cup and splashes on the floor.

Finally the teapot is empty and the horrified pilgrim places it on the table. At this point the teacher tells him: "You are like that teacup. You are so full you cannot take in anything more. You must first empty yourself if you wish to learn from me."

Days when your journal entry is rich and full can be exciting and satisfying. At the same time, it is important to appreciate the gift of days when your word cup is empty and you are open to the words of others.

There are probably as many approaches to journal writing as there are personality styles in the world, and this is reflected in the myriad of books available on the topic. If you are looking for a book to help you explore and develop your journal style, I recommend Lucia Capacchione's wonderful book, *The Creative Journal*.

A Pleasant Journey to Your Memory Bank
Identifying the activities and everyday experiences that you most enjoy and appreciate is a pleasant way to begin exploring and strengthening your connection to your Authentic Self.

Just now as I was writing this, I realized that a treasured experiences I had not indulged in for a long time was to take a leisurely walk through the Denver Botanical Gardens near my home. My favorite part of the gardens is an alpine exhibit complete with miniature Arctic poppies, tiny cactus, and exquisite diminutive wildflowers that grow at high altitudes.

While my morning started out on a hectic note, thinking about visiting that alpine garden had a replenishing effect. I could actually feel my shoulders relaxing at the thought of the Lilliputian daisies and wild purple lilies framed by distant snow-covered peaks against a bright blue sky. Just thinking about what you love can sometimes be nourishing as it helps you reconnect with your Authentic Self.

The things you especially enjoy doing or experiencing are like little holograms, self-contained images of who you really are deep inside. Identifying these and subsequently reconnecting to them in thought or action will simultaneously strengthen your awareness and your appreciation of your Authentic Self. And, if you happen to be weary from too many outside obligations, worries, and chores of daily life as I was earlier today, doing this exercise will refresh you.

 One Small Step
Imagine that you have been given the opportunity to spend the next fifteen minutes in your personal Memory Bank reliving one or more pleasant or meaningful experiences you have enjoyed over the last year. Take a few moments now to enjoy reliving one of these experiences in your mind, savoring what you most enjoyed, and noticing what appeals to you about it.

Possibilities
• What experience or experiences would you choose to relive? (If you have trouble thinking of things that you want to recur, try identifying those that you would least dislike repeating.)

- Were any of these everyday occurrences?
- What are some activities that occur less frequently but which you would like to repeat in the future?

When considering what experience you would value repeating in your life, it is important to include those occurrences that you have enjoyed infrequently, as well as those you already encounter more often.

I asked Erin, a busy mother of two young children, what experiences and activities she especially valued and wanted to have continue in her life. Here are a few of the things she said:

> I like to watch sunsets from our living room window. I like to give my baby a bath. He loves the water, and his smile melts me. I like to go to high tea at the Brown Palace. I like to spend time alone with my husband.

Although some happen more often in her life than others, all of the above experiences represent the Authentic Erin, meaningful reflections of who she really is. Furthermore, even when she doesn't have time to engage in one of these favorite activities, thinking of them helps her connect with her sense of self.

You may want to carry this list with you so you can reread it whenever you want. It can serve as a mental bridge to the resources and potential comfort inherent in your Authentic Self as you manage daily responsibilities. This is particularly useful when you are under stress or when painful memories or fears about the future interfere with your ability to enjoy the present.

A Message from a Guardian Angel
Imagine that a wise and compassionate guardian angel has been sitting on your shoulder since you were born. You have not been aware of this presence up until now because angels are weightless. The angel's sole purpose has been to recognize and observe all of your positive personality strengths and virtuous beliefs about the world. This is not an angel in charge of producing self-criticism or blame!

One Small Step
For the next fifteen minutes, imagine that the angel is now dictating a list of your positive attributes through you. Writing down whatever comes to mind, make a list of what you think the angel would say.

 Possibilities
- Which personality traits do you value most and want to continue to influence your approach to life?
- Which virtues or positive beliefs do you value most and want to continue to influence your approach to life?

Once you have completed this exercise, take some time to contemplate what you wrote. What was it like to create the list? Perhaps even with the device of the imaginary guardian angel, you found it difficult to catalog your positive personality characteristics. If so, don't worry as this is not uncommon, particularly if you come from a family or culture where such self-acknowledgment is not encouraged.

Try imagining what worthwhile and good things another person who understands you and likes you would notice about you. Or you might find it more helpful to imagine what good things an understanding and kindly stranger would notice while watching a videotape depicting your life. And be sure to start the list by noting your modesty! Once you have created the list, take a moment to consider any attributes or virtues that you may have overlooked.

A bright and gifted scientific researcher who had taught at two universities, Belinda found herself stumped when she first attempted to imagine an angel dictating a list of positive personality qualities about her. Naming positive attributes seemed too much like "tooting her own horn," a form of conceit that she had been taught in her childhood was wrong.

In the Irish Catholic family where Belinda grew up, people who talked too highly of themselves were considered braggarts, and were ridiculed as being full of themselves. Furthermore, people who viewed themselves as pious or holy were considered to be self-righteous phonies. For Belinda, imagining an angel saying positive things about her was egotistical and felt too close to boasting.

Despite ridiculing any form of self-praise, Belinda's family advocated complimenting other people, especially those who were absent or lived outside the immediate family circle.

As a result, a more comfortable and acceptable way for Belinda to identify her positive personality traits was to imagine the words that a caring friend might use to describe her. By supposing what her best friend, Sarah, might say, Belinda came up with the following list:

> Belinda is a good listener; she cares about other people's feelings.
> Belinda has a good sense of humor. Belinda is a careful and
> conscientious worker. Belinda is a loyal friend.

If, like Belinda, identifying positive personality traits about yourself was initially difficult or uncomfortable, chances are you have been taught that directly expressing positive feelings about yourself is unacceptable. Or perhaps you suffered psychological abuse and were thereby given the message that you did not deserve to feel good about yourself. Regardless of the cause, having difficulty identifying and acknowledging positive qualities and characteristics about yourself indicates that it is time to reclaim this ability.

Just as the activities and experiences that you value repeating in your life are an externally visible expression of your Authentic Self, so personality traits, inner virtues, or positive beliefs about the world are an internal expression of who you really are.

Alone or combined with the list of activities you developed in the Memory Bank exercise, your list of positive characteristics and traits can be reread whenever you need to bolster your courage or find support from within. This will help you connect more deeply to your Authentic Self while strengthening good feelings about yourself.

The next exercise will help you identify some of your beliefs and philosophy about life that characterize your Authentic Self. This exercise is adapted from one in *Writing for Your Life* by Deena Metzger.

The Last Fifteen Minutes of the World

Imagine that you have been gifted at birth with two things: the ability to express yourself well and some special knowledge to give the world. Unfortunately, you have not known of these abilities until now. You have also just learned that a terrible destructive force is about to hit the earth. This destructive force will destroy all libraries, museums, computers, and other information storage systems. Only those objects and that information placed in a special time capsule will survive.

 One Small Step

You are asked to contribute to the time capsule. Write, draw, or orally record your special information to help the human race survive after the catastrophe. You have only fifteen minutes to do this.

It is important that you limit yourself to just fifteen minutes so the process is spontaneous and does not become belabored. Whether you choose to write, draw, or orally record your response, it is also a good idea to preserve your response in some way, so that you can take time afterward to explore what the words reveal about your Authentic Self at this juncture in your life.

No two responses to this exercise will be alike. Since your Authentic Self is constantly growing, changing, and evolving, your responses are likely to vary somewhat on different occasions. Here is a portion of the response I wrote while writing this book:

> We must remember to expect, anticipate, and notice the inevitable good things, small or large, that also happen as part of daily life. It is better to live a life focused upon and influenced by the awareness of good things than the fear of bad things.

Remember that there is no wrong response to this exercise. It is also important to allow yourself to respond with humor if that is what you feel when doing the exercise.

When participating in one of my workshops, Ron found himself laughing aloud because the first thing he had written for the imaginary time capsule was: "Don't sit in the Poison Ivy." He had thoughtfully illustrated this suggestion with a drawing of the little three-leafed poisonous plant.

Not sitting in poison ivy was eminently sensible advice, and when he considered it on a metaphorical level, Ron found it to be an important reminder from his Authentic Self about needing to pay attention to the obvious in life, something he had been neglecting recently.

Whatever your response to the exercise, appreciate what it tells you about your Authentic Self's beliefs and philosophy.

Telling Your Life Story
Writing or orally recording your autobiography is another way to explore and deepen a connection with your Authentic Self. Depending on the amount of detail you want to include, creating your story may take hours, days, weeks, or longer. After you have written it, read it again and add details until you are satisfied that you have included all that is important to you.

In writing your story, beware of perfectionism! Remember that the purpose is to learn more about your Authentic Self by describing the events and experiences that have been significant to you. Some people find it easier to write an autobiography if they start by focusing on a particular theme such as "Houses I Have Lived In," "Important People in My Life," "Schools I Attended," "Pets I Have Loved," "Trips I Have Taken," "Treasured Friendships," and other topics uniquely significant to them.

If you are having a hard time beginning despite focusing on a theme, you might like to try the following exercise.

> **One Small Step**
> Give yourself three minutes to tell the story of your life. After three minutes, notice what you have written and decide whether you want to continue for another three minutes.

Because it is a nearly impossible and somewhat absurd task, this exercise often loosens the constrictions of self-imposed perfectionism and allows your Authentic Self to speak more freely.

A Time Line

If you wish to tell your story but do not want to do it as a narrative, try creating a Time Line.

 One Small Step

Find a quiet place to sit and think. You will need paper and pencil.

1. Draw a vertical line down the middle of a sheet of paper. On the upper left-hand corner write the word *birth* and your date of birth. Now list other demographic information about yourself such as approximate dates of starting school, moves, birth(s) of siblings, and so on in chronological order. Add information as it comes to you, including both pleasant and unpleasant information that you deem significant.
2. Record past or current feelings about each event in the space across from it on the right-hand side of the vertical line.

One page will probably not be enough. You may think of additional information that needs to be inserted to retain a chronological order to your Time Line. Just cut the paper horizontally and tape together additional strips of paper to insert new text. You may continue using paper and tape to form one long strip of paper that you can roll up and store in the form of a long scroll.

CREATING A SYMBOL FOR YOUR AUTHENTIC SELF

Words are not the only way to explore and connect more completely with your Authentic Self. Some people find it more meaningful to create a symbol or series of symbols that help them identify, explore, and further develop who they really are deep within.

A Coat of Arms

If you were to create a Coat of Arms to represent your Authentic Self what images would you include? What colors best represent who you are? Would you include things that represent your accomplishments, your hobbies, and other things you like to do?

Is there a saying or a logo that you would include in the form of an inscription or a banner? Notice what comes to mind.

You will need blank paper; drawing, coloring, or painting supplies; glue; and some old magazines or newspapers for this exercise.

One Small Step

Draw a Coat of Arms for yourself on a sheet of paper and notice what emerges. Feel free to add images cut out from newspapers and magazines, as well as objects from nature such as discarded feathers, bits of dried wood, or flowers. Remember that the idea in creating a Coat of Arms is to learn more about your Authentic Self. Don't worry if your creation is not great art!

Brad was just doodling when he began his Coat of Arms. He was sitting in a little cafe waiting for a friend, and found himself playfully drawing the image of a feather on the back of his cardboard notebook.

He noticed himself drawing another feather and realized that, although he had not deliberately drawn a picture since high school art class, he had been drawing these feathers for years when he was talking on the phone, sitting at meetings, or waiting for people to arrive. They were definitely part of him.

He began to wonder what other symbols or objects reflected who he really was, and as he waited for his friend he began to add other doodles to the back of his notebook. To his surprise many of the things he added were shapes and images he associated with the Native American culture.

Although Brad is one-eighth Cherokee on his grandfather's side, he had not understood how significant this aspect of his heritage was until he drew his Coat of Arms. Brad found that exploring his Cherokee background further through books and interviewing tribal elders was a meaningful path to his Authentic Self.

An Animal Symbol

If you could be any animal, what would you choose to be? Chances are your choice says something about your Authentic Self.

One Small Step
Draw a picture of this animal, and then write a description of the animal's special characteristics and habits. What qualities do you find most appealing about this animal?

Now imagine that you are in fact the animal you have selected, and take some time to imagine yourself as this animal. How would you spend a typical day? What do you like and dislike about being this animal?

Louise named a rabbit as her favorite animal, imagining a large, light brown jack-rabbit that she had seen in her childhood when she was growing up in a small Arizona desert town.

She described the rabbit as quiet and shy. In thinking about rabbits she recognized they are resourceful because "you have to be when you are that small and vulnerable." In imagining a typical day in the life of a rabbit, she noted that rabbits burrow in the earth and they're vegetarian. If necessary they will use their sharp claws to defend themselves and their babies. A rabbit knows how to take care of herself.

In identifying with the rabbit, Louise realized some valuable things about herself: she was resourceful; she could take care of herself; and though shy, she was capable of defending or protecting herself.

After doing this exercise, Louise placed an image of a rabbit on her desk as a way to further connect and identify with her Authentic Self. What object or picture would help you identify with the animal you chose for this exercise?

A Tree That Speaks to You
This exercise needs to be done when you have time to walk around outdoors in a wooded setting. The tree is a device upon which you can project your thoughts, feelings, and special awareness, thereby allowing your Authentic Self to speak to you.

One Small Step
Give yourself a minimum of an hour to walk around and contemplate various trees. Look for a tree that you find particularly appealing. Imagine that this

tree has something to tell you about your Authentic Self. Imagine that the tree knows something important about you because you are kindred spirits. Ask the tree to tell you how you are alike, and write down what comes to mind. Then ask the tree to tell you the message it has for you about your Authentic Self, and write down whatever you imagine the tree tells you.

Here is the response that came to me while I contemplated a tall ponderosa pine in a mountain meadow:

> You and I are alike because we have stood in the same place for a long while, enduring snow and rain and drought. Because we endured we know we can survive the winter to come and the hot summer days that will follow again next year. On a typical day I watch the sunrise, listen to the bird songs, feel the wind against my branches, and take special joy in seeing the sunset give way to a sky full of stars. The special message I have for you is to notice the grand blue sky above you and the beautiful clouds it harbors, and also the wildflowers, squirrels, and hummingbirds beneath it. Enjoying what is here with you right now is important. You spend too much time worrying and not enough time allowing yourself to enjoy the moment.

This exercise can be repeated on various walks in the future, choosing whatever tree appeals to you on each walk.

Totem Dolls

Historically, doll making has been practiced to develop nurturing and maturity. Young girls in Africa once made fertility dolls for themselves as a preparation for puberty, marriage, and childbearing. In many different traditions, dolls have been made for spiritual purposes.

Inspired in part by African tribal dolls, and borrowing ideas from Native American totem poles and European coats of arms, I began experimenting with what has evolved into Totem Dolls. A Totem Doll can be whatever size you wish. You can attach whatever articles you feel symbolize who you are.

A Totem Doll can be used to represent who you were, who you are, and who you wish to become. One doll can represent the various aspects of your life, or if you prefer, you can make different dolls for the past, the present, and the future.

 One Small Step

Sew a doll by machine or by hand and decorate it with buttons, beads, paper, or whatever objects represent you. Books with instructions for making small and large dolls are readily obtained from fabric and craft shops and libraries. These instructions can be adapted to make your own self-expressive dolls.

Don't be intimidated by the idea of making a Totem Doll to represent yourself. On the wall of the room where I do most of my creative work, I have tacked a small sign:

Show me a person who never made a mistake, and I'll show you a person who never made anything!

Loose stitches and less-than-perfect craftsmanship only add to the charm and evocative personality of a homemade Totem Doll representing your Authentic Self.

As an alternative to sewing a doll, you can contact a doll maker and commission a clay doll that represents an aspect of your inner self. Look at examples of the doll maker's work to ensure that the doll will reflect your style. Ask the doll maker to draw a model of the doll before constructing it to ensure that the resulting doll is what you had in mind.

Even easier and less costly is making a paper Totem Doll. In *Reclaiming Herstory*, Cheryl Bell-Gadsby and Ann Siegenberg suggest decorating paper dolls to symbolize one's self. The paper dolls can be decorated in the same manner as the fabric Totem Dolls. However, they are more fragile, and some people find they are not as personally evocative as three-dimensional cloth or clay dolls.

Susan, a woman who had suffered a painful knee operation included a gash of red fabric across the knee of her doll. Since she had grown up in the north woods and had loved the forest as a child, she also included a piece of pine bark in the doll's stuffing.

She then added items to symbolize her current self. These included a symbolic wedding band sewn to the doll's hand, a miniature book with the names of her three children written inside it, and a small bag labeled "Manure" that symbolized some of the political corruption she was dealing with in her work at a major corporation. (The bag did not contain real manure for obvious aesthetic and olfactory reasons!)

To represent her future self, Susan drew some attractive wrinkles with a piece of grey chalk. She added some white strands to the brown string she had used to depict her hair. She added another bag, affixed to the dolls waist, and labeled it "Free Time." On a small piece of paper rolled up like a scroll, she wrote "MBA," symbolizing achievement of the graduate degree she was pursuing.

Susan is twenty years younger than her husband and fears he will die before her. To reflect her future grief over his death, she tied a small piece of black fabric around the doll's upper arm. The fabric was torn, not cut, so that the raw edges would reflect the raw feelings she anticipates. On top of the miniature book with her children's names, she tied a second book. Inside this one she wrote "Memories of Good Times with Jim," which she knows will comfort her sometime in the future.

Maggie responded to the Totem Doll exercise by first making a small doll that represented her as a child. Marks on the doll's head represented emotional abuse she had endured, and marks on its body symbolized other kinds of abuse.

A piece of wavy blue paper depicted the ocean and sand she had loved as a child, and a yellow bead symbolized the cherished accompanying sun. Seashells worked naturally as articles of clothing for this doll. As a little girl, Maggie had fantasized that she was a mermaid.

To symbolize the present, Maggie made a larger doll to remind herself she is older, bigger, and less vulnerable than the mermaid child. She cut out words from magazines and pasted them directly on the doll to describe various virtues and faults she saw as being true of her present self.

She also added articles to reflect activities she enjoys—a sprig of dried herb to reflect her love of cooking, a piece of an old shoelace to remember her daily jogging. It was not until she was drawing a mouth on her Present Doll that she realized her smaller, younger doll had no mouth. As a child she had been mute in her pain. Now, she added a mouth to the Past Doll to represent her personal healing and growth.

It was several weeks before Maggie felt ready to make a doll representing the future. She decided to make it out of the same cloth as the other two dolls, since it represented a continuation of the self. But she wanted this doll to look older, as she would be in the future. She dipped the remaining fabric in strong brewed tea to make it look more aged. Then she glued on two stars for eyes to signify the wisdom of age.

Tickled by the idea that she would allow herself to be more expressive and even eccentric when she was old, Maggie visited toy stores and looked at commercial doll clothes until she found a hat that she could decorate with a bright red rose and a small paper butterfly. Maggie does not consider her Future Doll completed, and may well add things to it for many years to come. I asked her, "What will you do if your Future Doll becomes too small for all the things you want to add to it?"

She smiled and answered:

> Then I will make a bigger Future Doll and before I stuff it, I will put this doll inside it, so it is an integral part of the new doll. I might fasten some of the things from this doll on the bigger one, or I might just leave them inside. What is important is that *I* know they are in there.

Other Creative Paths

Dancing; writing poetry, stories, or plays; painting; drawing; quilting; singing—the creative paths to your Authentic Self are endless. The best guide is what appeals to you. If you long for further exploration but are not sure what you want to do, try devoting several weekly "artist's dates" to considering your creative side.

In *The Artist's Way*, Julia Cameron suggests making a weekly artist's date with yourself. This date consists of setting aside an hour and a half or longer to pursue activities you would not normally get to experience, time simply to explore the creative aspect of your Authentic Self. You might take a class; visit museums, exhibitions, or art supply stores; or experiment with following your own whims. Don't be daunted by the "critic within." Most creative people proceed despite an inner critic.

Especially when practiced on a regular basis, scheduling time for your artistic interests can be a powerful and rewarding way to foster a connection with that aspect of your Authentic Self that is the source of all your creative pursuits.

CONNECTING TO YOUR AUTHENTIC SELF
THROUGH RELAXATION AND PLAY

There are many ways to reconnect with and explore your Authentic Self. Some of the most powerful techniques are also some of the most enjoyable—times we spend resting and recreating.

Taking Time to Just Be

Perhaps you already give yourself permission to spend a few minutes each day just letting yourself "be." If so, you are a rare person, as many of us in Western society live frenetic lives. The gift of fifteen or twenty minutes a day of unstructured time in which you quietly rest, contemplate, or allow your mind to wander is a rewarding way to connect to your Authentic Self. An enjoyable way to approach this time is to notice where in your body you feel most comfortable and to allow that comfort to spread to the rest of your body.

Taking a Mini-Vacation

It took me a long time to recognize the difference in myself between being exhausted and being lazy or depressed. Many times in the past, I would find myself without energy. Inevitably, I would accuse myself of being lazy or diagnose myself as depressed. The antidote for these things, I had been taught, was structure and activity. And so I would make a list of productive things to do that day, and proceed to do them as efficiently as possible.

The next day, like clockwork, I would become ill. Usually it was characterized by a fever and flu symptoms that kept me in bed for a day or more. More recently, I have learned to take some time off to rest when I begin to experience the state I once labeled as laziness or depression.

Last week I had just such a day. Once the essential things were done (bathing, brushing my teeth, feeding my pets, returning a few phone calls), I allowed myself to take a mini-vacation. I began by drinking tea by the fireplace. I napped, listened to good music, embroidered the face on a rag doll, caught up on some reading, telephoned several friends, and ended with a long, luxurious bubble bath. After a few hours, I emerged refreshed and energized. Today I feel fine.

If you already spend a lot of unstructured time, taking time off may merely be redundant and not particularly useful. In this case, activity may be a better means to self-renewal. However, if you tend to be very active and are now feeling stale or tired, you may benefit from a taking a few hours off in which you just let yourself be. Furthermore, it may prevent you from becoming ill.

Possibilities

- If you were to take a mini-vacation, would it be characterized by rest and quiet relaxation like mine, or would it be more active and involve leaving your accustomed environment for a few hours?

Focusing Your Attention

Focusing your attention on the present is a natural way to connect with and more vividly experience your Authentic Self. We are born with this ability, and we see it in young children, but unfortunately most people are robbed of it during the journey to adulthood.

Yesterday afternoon in the supermarket, I saw a small girl holding a mango in her hand as she sat quietly in her mother's grocery cart. She was oblivious of her surroundings, and her face held an expression of rapt attention. With the wonderful lack of self-consciousness inherent in young children, her fingers prodded, squeezed, and stroked the surface of the rosy mango as if she was trying to learn all the secrets of "mango-ness."

Preoccupied with phone calls I needed to return and letters I had to write, I had been hurrying through the market intent on finishing the chore of grocery shopping as quickly as possible. Seeing that wonderful little girl stopped me in my tracks. She was at that moment happily living in the estate of her Authentic Self. Clearly I was not.

I had been traversing the market at record speed but proceeding on automatic pilot, my mind elsewhere. I had not even registered the symphony of jewel-like shapes and colors in the well-stocked summer produce market. I had missed out on the exquisite sunset color of the ripening peaches, the wine-colored raspberries, and the crimson cherries, all of their scents mingling agreeably with the soothing aroma of fresh-baked bread. After seeing that little girl, I resolved to slow down and focus on the moment.

One Small Step
Take a moment now to notice the shapes, colors, smells, and textures around you. Focus on what you are experiencing as you do so.

An Ericksonian Relaxation Method

The Ericksonian Relaxation Method (Dolan, 1991) helps you reclaim your natural ability to enjoy the moment that painful or traumatic experiences disrupted. This method is also a good way to nurture yourself during or after a hectic day, and can be used to . encourage sleep at night.

This is a very powerful technique, so please read all the instructions before proceeding with the exercise. Under no circumstances should this exercise be done while driving a car or using machinery.

 One Small Step
Find a comfortable position in which your body feels well supported. Focus your gaze on some pleasant or restful view. Nature is often an enjoyable choice. If you find yourself in a jarring or unrelaxing environment, you might prefer to simply gaze at a pretty postcard or some other object you like that you place in front of you. It doesn't matter what you choose to look at, as long as it is not disturbing. Or you may want to look at an uncluttered wall.

Concentrating only on what you are viewing, name five things that you see. Now name five things that you hear, and name five physical sensations you are aware of.

(Don't worry if you can't think of five different things in each category. It's fine to repeat the same thing more than once; for example, "I see the tree. I still see the tree." Everything you name is to be something you see in front of you from your present position.)

Once you have named five items for each category, name four items for each category, that is, four sights, four sounds, four physical sensations. Continue by naming three items in each category, two in each category, and one in each category.

When you reach one, you can either continue the process by starting again with five items per category or simply stop and enjoy the sensation of vividly experiencing the moment. If you get confused or lose your place before you reach one, simply stop and enjoy the sense of deep relaxation and communion with your Authentic Self.

If you are very tired when you are doing this, you may fall asleep. In fact, it can be used as a way to relax into sleep by repeating it until you drift off. If you are doing this to get to sleep in a darkened room with little to see, you may want to simply repeat, "I see the darkened space in front of me" for the visual category. As an alternative, if you prefer to keep your eyes closed, you could choose to skip the sights category.

When using this method, feel free to stop at any time as you progress from five to one items, and simply enjoy the experience of fully connecting to what you see, hear, and feel in the present moment.

For some hypnotically gifted individuals, doing this exercise will result in a light hypnotic trance. This is an example of the common everyday trance that occurs natural- ly when people become pleasantly absorbed in an everyday experience like watching an excellent movie, looking at a beautiful sunset, or enjoying a mango like the little girl in the supermarket.

If at any time during or after the exercise, you want to become more focused and alert, the easiest way to shift away from such wide attention is to physically move. Stand up and walk around. If you are feeling sleepy or spacey and wish to shift back to a more alert state, you can also count yourself back into alertness: (1) I am more and more alert and refreshed; (2) I am even more alert; (3) I am even more refreshed and alert; (4) I am even more refreshed; (5) I am fully alert and refreshed.

After doing this relaxation exercise, take some time to simply rest and to connect with your Authentic Self.

This chapter has offered a wide range of possibilities to help you reclaim and further enjoy the estate of your Authentic Self. Return to the sections that best nurture and replenish you. The next chapter will invite you to continue and further develop this process of coming home to your Authentic Self by exploring ways to enhance your quality of everyday life in your home environment.

CHAPTER TWO

WELCOME HOME!

If there is harmony in the house
There will be order in the nation.
If there is order in the nation
There will be peace in the world.

—Chinese Proverb

After a good dinner, one can forgive anybody, even one's own relatives.

—Oscar Wilde

As a reflection of the people who live there, home is a natural symbol for yourself and your beliefs about how life should be lived. Spending time at home engaged in simple and cozy activities has recently become a national trend in America as evidenced by the popularity of magazines devoted to cooking, crafts, decorating, and other homey pursuits.

Divided into four sections, this chapter introduces suggestions—small celebrations, favorite decorative choices, pleasing room arrangements, and challenging a prosperity mind-set—to increase your pleasure and ease in your home right now.

GREETING EVERYDAY GIFTS

This chapter invites you to explore various ways to enhance the quality of your everyday life at home. When first exploring these ideas, some people, particularly those who have suffered childhood abuse or neglect, find themselves questioning whether they deserve good things in their home life on a daily basis. When asked to envision how she could enhance the quality of her everyday life, Connie, a business manager at a busy medical office, had the following response:

Working on creating a home that pleases me, establishing daily rituals just to make myself feel good, are ideas that would have been considered trivial or even selfish in the family where I grew up. I mean, it's like giving myself a gift every day for no reason at all. Do I really deserve this?

A month later Connie had a different perspective:

After the first few weeks of doing these things, I realized that my self-nurturing at home was having a ripple effect. Because my own needs were being met, I was more patient and tolerant with my family and other people both at home and at work. My relationships were improving.

Regardless of whether being good to yourself was encouraged in your childhood, and perhaps even more so if it was not, you have a right to experience life-affirming personal rituals and a pleasant place to live. Keep in mind that nurturing yourself will increase, not decrease, your ability to nurture others.

Nurturing Daily Rituals

When I was a young girl there was a part of the weekday that never varied. I would come home from school at four o'clock, and my mother would be sitting at the table drinking a cup of tea. A friend would usually be visiting with her, but even if she was alone, she would stop and give herself that time of respite before starting dinner.

Often I would join her. The little room where she always took her tea looked out on an old pear tree, and this marked the seasons of our tea drinking. I remember her laughing one fall afternoon as she described watching our fat old cat leaping around under that pear tree, trying to catch each leaf as it dropped to the ground.

The pear tree's branches became bare against the grey winter sky then lit up again with pale spring blossoms and the promise of birds that would come in summer to eat the ripe pears that had fallen to the ground. Drinking tea was a small and ordinary daily ceremony for my mother, yet it added a reassuring continuity to my life, and I suspect to hers also. Our family moved many times over the years, and the tea drinking may have eased the transitions by providing a reassuring constancy in the daily patterns of our household.

These days, like my mother, I stop whatever I am doing at four o'clock. But it is for a different ceremony than drinking tea. I stand at the edge of the garden and listen. After a moment I hear the hoofbeats of wild elk running down the valley on their way to the pond. Soon I see them approaching and watch entranced as they leap playfully over wildflowers and pine seedlings then pass out of sight over the hill. It seems that they too have predictable daily patterns.

In our modern world with its frantic pace, simple rituals that bestow comfort have become increasingly important. While such practices naturally vary from person to person, they share the common purpose of humanizing and enriching one's daily life.

I enjoy observing the rituals of daily life around me. My friend Linda does yoga every morning. David begins his morning with a cup of fragrant tea. Paula takes stock of what her garden needs before she leaves for work and looks forward all day to working in the soil that evening. Gardening helps her deal with the ups and downs of everyday life. She says her grandmother was the same way and would take out her garden hoe whenever she was upset about something, working things out in her mind as she worked the earth.

Mark and Julie take a walk together in the foothills every morning before going to work. Taking cut flowers from his garden to work brings Michael a sense of peacefulness on the job. Charlie takes a few minutes during his working hours to play solitaire on his computer. He emerges refreshed and relaxed and continues his work tasks with renewed creativity.

Steve takes a nightly walk just before going to bed. Luke listens to classical music on Sunday morning while ironing his shirts for the week. Insoo finds it calming and centering to clean her house. Several people told me that cleaning and reorganizing closets and drawers relaxes them, providing something to do while mentally exploring and clarifying thoughts and creative ideas.

Most mornings, before reading the newspaper or talking to anyone, my husband goes outdoors and feeds the wild birds who congregate outside our kitchen window. He then spends a few minutes quietly sipping his coffee and listening to their songs and conversations. My cat sits and stares dreamily at the fire for a while every night.

Marilyn spends an hour each night doing needlepoint while she watches the evening news. The rhythmic stitches remind her to slow down and enjoy the moments of her life. When her three children were teenagers, needlepoint helped her cope with the stress of adolescence and gave her a much-needed respite of peace and quiet as she waited up for them at night. Although her children have now grown into responsible adults, Marilyn still benefits from her evening needlepoint ritual. With each stitch her breathing becomes more calm and even. After an hour her hands and eyes are tired and her mind is relaxed.

A busy accountant with a high-pressured schedule, Michael runs each morning wherever he is regardless of weather or climate. While most people exercise to benefit their body, Michael does it to enhance his mental functioning later in the day. He says that running early in the morning clears the cobwebs out of his mind, and he feels more alert all day.

For several years Debra and her women friends have shared the magic of a monthly walk in the mountain forest under the full moon. They have done this in soft spring rain, blowing snow, on tranquil summer nights, and in every other imaginable kind of weather. The effect is always one of wonder at the beauty of nature, and a renewed appreciation of the friendship they share.

Angela burns a stick of delicately perfumed sandalwood incense every night just before she goes to bed, careful to keep it contained in a safe holder. She loves the experience of drifting off to sleep while inhaling the exquisite fragrance and awakening to its subtle scent still lingering throughout the house.

Louise, a busy mother of seven school-age children, tells me she makes time to quilt a little each evening. She is often too tired to relax completely enough to just sit quietly in the evening and rest, even though she knows that would be good for her. But the needle and thread in her hand allow her to transition from intense busyness to a sense of tranquillity.

Kerry picks up a novel at night for the same reason that Louise quilts at the end of the day. People I interviewed about their nurturing rituals often described nightly reading as an important part of their lives. Several explained that when stressed, they found "trying" to relax enough to fall asleep generally increased their restlessness, but reading for a few minutes provided an effortless transition into a restful state.

What they chose to read before sleep varied. But we should consciously select the books we read or TV shows we watch late at night since the content of what we hear or see just before falling asleep can affect our dreams.

Carla stretches each night for several minutes before going to bed. She says these movements simultaneously quiet her mind and relax her body. Before she started stretching she used to awaken in the morning with stiff muscles. Now she gets out of bed with ease, ready to greet the day.

Writing is an important ritual for me. I have kept a journal for more than twenty years. If more than a few days pass without taking time for the journal, I become restless and irritable. I have written on crowded buses and trains, while riding in a dugout canoe on a swampy river in a Central American rainforest, inside primitive thatched huts, and in elegant European tearooms. The effect is always the same: a renewed sense of contact with my inner self, an appreciation for the world around me, and an accompanying peacefulness.

Possibilities
- What are your nurturing daily rituals?
- What daily ceremonies have you observed in others that appeal to you?
- Do you want to incorporate any of these into your own life? If so, choose one that is especially appealing or create one of your own, and experiment with it this week.

The Comfort of Food
Food can be a comforting experience as well as a ritual of celebration. Despite the advent of trends toward low-fat cooking, fast food popularity, and take-out food, and our increased gastronomic sophistication in this age of ethnically varied global cuisine, people continue to crave the simple foods of their childhood—home-style cooking, also called comfort food.

Holly remembers a difficult time at age ten when her mother was hospitalized for cancer and wavered for several days near death. A housekeeper, Mrs. Robinson, was hired to manage the house, cook, and care for Holly and her two younger sisters.

Almost immediately she began preparing all of the children's favorite foods, the same ones their mother usually cooked. This brought a much-needed sense of comfort and reassurance. Years later Holly asked Mrs. Robinson how she knew which were their favorite foods.

Mrs. Robinson smiled:

> That was easy. I just opened your mother's cookbook and found the pages that had food stains. The more food stains, I figured the more you liked the recipe.

Last year, while teaching a seminar in Belgium, I stayed at the home of a colleague who lives in the small village that was the ancestral home of my great-grandmother. Tired at the end of the day, I decided to take a nap before dinner. I awakened with a pervasive feeling of well-being.

I soon identified the source of my good feelings. The fragrances wafting from the kitchen up to my room were familiar ones, the same ones I had smelled many times in my grandmother's kitchen! My host, a gifted cook, had prepared a local Belgian dish. The same recipe must have traveled across the ocean with Great-Grandmother Flavia and been faithfully passed on to her daughter.

Possibilities
- What foods do you associate with comfort and well-being?
- Are these part of your current life? If not, might they be a source of comfort or reassurance during stressful times?

When I interviewed people about what they associated with rituals of celebration, many described special foods, cloth napkins, and candles on the table. Some people mentioned costly foods and beverages: champagne, caviar, lobster. But not all food associated with festive occasions is costly. Some foods remembered from similarly happy occasions evoke feelings of celebration.

For Kathleen, it wouldn't be Thanksgiving without her mother's chestnut stuffing. Keith notes wryly that while he hates the Midwestern tradition of "suspending previously canned fruits in bowls of surrealistically colored gelatin," it wouldn't be Christmas without his grandmother Delores's canned apricot-studded lime Jell-O salad. And so he makes one every year, much to the amusement and mock horror of his partner.

You can start your own new traditions. As a teenager, because I loved the fragrance and taste of gingerbread, I began to bake gingerbread boys at Christmas for the rest of my family. I have now been baking gingerbread every winter for thirty years. Although this was not a tradition passed down to me by any relative, it has become a meaningful one for me.

Other foods that were not part of my childhood but which have become my personal traditions over the past fifteen years are a spicy Southwestern Chocolate Bread Pudding and a New Orleans Chicken Andouille Gumbo. I serve these at various festive family gatherings, and friends have been known to phone ahead to make sure I am including them on the menu! For me, *family* means close friends as well as relatives.

While starting new traditions may feel a little odd at first, there can be many advantages to doing this. Healthier or more colorful and appealing food that you introduce as a new tradition can become a positive legacy to your descendants.

If your family of origin tended to act out pain, violence, or other forms of dysfunction during holiday gatherings, the traditional foods you associate with those occasions may induce sadness. In this case, introducing new foods or food preparations to your celebrations can be especially valuable. Preparing and serving food that is special but different than what your family ate can help you move beyond painful past memories and establish new and positive mental associations with future holidays. And as you prepare and serve your own special foods on holidays over the course of several years, these dishes will take on a meaningful aura of ritual and tradition.

If you would like to establish new food traditions for your own holidays and special occasions and want further ideas, ethnic cookbooks from various countries can be an interesting resource. Traditional ethnic cooking is based on culinary wisdom that evolved according to the availability of various ingredients in the locale where it developed. This has resulted in some very appealing traditional dishes.

Contemporary cookbooks that feature light and healthy food can also be a useful source of new ideas. Select from various customs that interest you as you further create and evolve your own traditions.

Possibilities
- What observances do you most associate with festive occasions?
- Are there new foods you would enjoy introducing into future holidays or other seasonal special celebrations?
- Would you enjoy exploring new ideas from cookbooks or friends' recipe files?
- What might be the first step to creating a new tradition of your own for a festive occasion?

SURROUNDING YOURSELF WITH WHAT YOU LOVE

Your home is your private sanctuary and should be aesthetically pleasing as well as functional. Decorate your walls and floors and countertops with your favorite colors and textures. Display your favorite objects. Create your own sense of beauty.

Painting the Walls and More
What colors lift your spirits? Do you love warm colors or cool ones? Do you find pastels soothing? Are you invigorated and refreshed by bright, intense saturated colors? Or do you prefer the serenity of a monochromatic color scheme warmed by touches of wood? Perhaps you prefer the restful tones of neutral colors such as shades of white, black, grey, or tan.

Since childhood, I have been crazy about the combination of bright blue and yellow. Just before I began to write this, I was out in my backyard garden cutting stems of intense yellow moonglow yarrow and placing them in small cobalt blue glass jars and bottles I have collected over many years.

Unfortunately a population of tiny insects love the moonglow yarrow as much as I do, so I have to wash each flower individually before bringing them into the house. It's a laborious process, but worth it because of the delight I feel every time I walk into the kitchen and feast my eyes on the dozens of little blue-and-yellow bouquets that line the window sills. Why do I go to all this trouble? Simply because it makes me happy.

- 44 -

Possibilities
- What colors, objects, textures, furniture, and other belongings do you associate with well-being?
- How could you introduce aspects of these into your home environment?
- What would be the first small step?

There are many ways to introduce the colors you love into your home. Althea collects pieces of beautiful fabric in her favorite colors and drapes them around her house to delight her eyes. She explains, "This is how I store fabrics!" Some fabrics are sewn into garments or linens. Others are left attractively draped for years or are given away to friends, relatives, or Goodwill when Althea tires of them. She has hung curtain rods not only across windows but throughout her house and enjoys draping fabrics on these for variety and pleasure as well as the privacy they provide.

Walking along the Pacific Ocean near her home, Samantha literally stumbled on a piece of beautiful green glass. It was her favorite shade of green. Its once-jagged edges had been rounded, polished by the sand and water. She fell in love with the soft green tones of the glass and began to look for additional pieces during her daily walks on the beach. Her house is now decorated with many pieces of beautiful polished green glass, all gifts from the sea.

Joanna enjoys many different colors and loves them all with gusto! In spring and summer she is drawn to restful pastels. When the leaves begin to turn in the New England village where she lives, she craves russets, golds, and browns, and in the winter she says with her typical enthusiasm, "I just can't get enough red!"

Although she is not a wealthy woman, Joanna has found a way to satisfy her large and varied appetite for color. The interior of her small house is neutral with white walls. Her few pieces of furniture are covered with washable cream-colored slipcovers. The covers on the throw pillows that adorn the furniture and the cloth that covers her kitchen table, however, change with the seasons.

Paint is a time-honored way to add color to a home. A decorator observed that in proportion to the effects achieved, a can of paint may be one of the best bargains for introducing change into your living environment. Furthermore, some paint and hardware stores sell unclaimed, rejected, or leftover custom-mixed paints at extremely discounted prices. But paint doesn't need to be limited to walls.

My friend Richard loves purple. One day he took a paintbrush and playfully painted small details in a beautiful shade of purple in unexpected places throughout his living space. Then he walked outdoors and added touches to the outside of his house and garage as well.

One of the last touches he added was the word, "Yes!" written in purple paint. Whenever I visit his home, this expression of purple exuberance delights me. I imagine it cheers Richard and his wife and daughter on a daily basis.

My sister Laura especially loves vibrantly colored painted surfaces on furniture. The mother of a mischievous, very active young son, she knew that the fragile painted surfaces of the furniture she admired in galleries would not stand up to the wear and tear of his playtime. So she literally took matters into her own hands. Wanting to experiment with paint effects and designs, she began collecting old wooden chairs, tables, and cabinets so decrepit looking that no one else wanted them.

As her painting and designing skills developed, she redecorated some of her earliest pieces with fresh paint. She now lives in the colorfully painted folk art environment she once coveted, and no longer worries about the potential effects of her child's antics on the furniture. She can always touch it up!

Bringing Nature Indoors

Do you like the being surrounded by living things? Perhaps you find the constantly moving shapes of the colorful fish in an aquarium especially relaxing. Or maybe you prefer the four-footed affection of a faithful dog or cat. As my friend Diane once observed, "Cats are ever changing living soft sculpture." Actually, this is true of all living things. Some, like plants, hundred-year-old trees, and cactuses change more slowly than others.

Do plants comfort you in your living space? If you especially love the forest, perhaps you would enjoy having a living tree in your home. Or if you love the desert, a cactus could simulate the open spaces that soothe your soul. Green plants and trees help purify the air, while providing a calming leafy backdrop for all your everyday activities.

A couple I know live in the Rocky Mountains, but also love the ocean. Their bathroom shelves are filled with large and small seashells they have collected on beaches during various vacations. These things cost nothing but time, yet provide rich reminders of treasured vacations. Another similarly minded person has a picture of herself swimming with dolphins hanging in her office.

Possibilities
- What appeals to you outdoors?
- How might you evoke this in your home?

Delighting in Textures
Eighteen-month-old Daniel squeals with delight when his toes touch velvet. Sammy, my cat, loves freshly laundered cotton. The moment he curls up on a quilt he signals his pleasure with loud purring. Texture is an often overlooked source of pleasure and comfort.

Possibilities
- Do you prefer smooth or rough textures?
- If you had your choice, would you select leather, wood, velvet, linen, cotton, or silk for a favorite chair?
- What sort of textures feel best to you?

If you're not sure what textures you like, walk through a fabric or upholstery store and let your fingers and eyes tell you which surfaces you find most appealing. Of course, at home the enjoyment of texture is not limited to your fingers and eyes.

Inside his Isla Negra home, the Chilean poet Pablo Neruda paved a hallway in small rounded stones specifically so he could enjoy the cobbled surface with his bare feet. In the primitive courtyard off our living room, I planted woolly thyme for the same reason Neruda arranged his stones, the pleasure it gives bare feet.

On a recent visit, my mother exclaimed over the softness of the much-washed cotton sheets I had used to make her bed. They reminded her of the long-ago feeling of her girlhood bed.

Sarah covered all her chairs with a patchwork of old linen fabrics, chosen less for color than for their cool feel during the hot, humid summers where she lives.

Alan collects baskets, especially favoring old ones in various stages of disrepair. He loves the look and feel of their worn surfaces, displaying them carefully on the wall where they can be touched as well as seen.

Mary chooses pottery cups and dishes specifically for their feel, preferring the look and heft of oddly shaped oversized pieces. Betsy swears her tea tastes better when she wraps her fingers around a thin porcelain cup.

The potential for enjoying texture in your home is as unlimited as your imagination. Let your hands, eyes, and creativity guide you as you take some time now to imagine how you might incorporate the textures that delight you into your home.

Art in Your Home
My husband and I bought art before we bought furniture, preferring to feast our eyes instead of cushioning our bodies. Even so, our taste often outstripped our budget. By necessity we learned to occasionally settle for signed posters and lithographs instead of original pieces by the artists we loved. Sometimes mass produced reproductions were the only way we could afford to introduce a particular artist's vision into our home.

When, as a young woman struggling to make ends meet, even posters were out of reach, I did what my grandmother and mother had done before me and looked for beauty wherever I could find it. Fortunately I didn't have to look far. Thanks to an extended family that always included small children, I have never been without their gifts of colorful and creative original finger paintings, drawings, and clay sculptures. Each one was a treasure conveying a unique and personal childhood world. As Picasso once said, "It takes a long time to see like a child."

But perhaps you like "grownup" art as well. If you are not yet sure what style of art most appeals to you, begin by visiting galleries and museums. A fun game to play with children and adults when visiting museums and galleries is to pretend that you will each be allowed to take home one piece of art. Deciding which piece you would choose when you visit an exhibition will help you explore and define your own taste in art.

Try to imagine yourself living with the piece over many years. How would it look in various rooms in your house? Never buy art under pressure, especially if it entails a sizable financial investment. If necessary, walk out of the gallery so you can contemplate your decision without the pressure of a salesperson.

If you love art but your current budget is tight, don't despair. You can sometimes purchase a piece over time, or possibly arrange with the artist to trade one of your skills for the artwork. If you live near a college or university, watch for the art department's yearly sales of works by talented students.

Nick loves good art and rejoiced when he finally moved into a spare, uncluttered house with lots of empty wall space for the framed original paintings he had always coveted. Unfortunately the style and quality of artwork Nick loves is currently beyond his budget. But the idea of coming home to bare walls every night for several years while saving up for one really good piece of art depressed him.

As an interim solution, Nick decided to display the postcard prints he had been collecting for years at numerous art museums. Individually matted and set in elegant old frames he had found at secondhand stores and refinished, the postcards portrayed some of the world's best art and reminded Nick of his favorite museums. Visitors to his house never guess that the elegant framed prints they are admiring are actually inexpensive postcards.

Choosing what you love is the best guideline to buying art. In order to "see" a painting, sculpture, or other piece of art over time it is helpful to move it occasionally so that it again captures your attention.

One Small Step
The first small step in adding art to your home is discovering what kind of art you love. Have you already begun?

ARRANGING AND REARRANGING YOUR HOME

The arrangement of furniture and other objects in your home should reflect and support your lifestyle. They should be functional—allowing you to relax, work, or entertain— but also attractive. But most of all, your home environment should nourish and revitalize your spirit.

The Ascetics of Order

As a young child I was influenced by my maternal grandmother's opinions about the ascetics of cleanliness and order. One day as she energetically scoured her kitchen sink, she told me:

> Vonnie, filth can transform a beautiful house into a trash heap, and cleanliness can bring a feeling of peacefulness and beauty to the most humble shack. Don't forget this.

Her manner indicated that she had shared an important secret, probably one she had learned from her own mother or grandmother. She viewed cleaning her house as a way not only of restoring but of creating peace and beauty. After hearing these ideas, I began making my bed first thing every morning and keeping my bedroom in good order, habits which have endured throughout my life. Though I didn't realize it until years later, Grandma had caused me to see the action of cleaning or tidying as a magical, alchemical activity that transforms an environment.

The functionality of cleanliness and order, the convenience of being easily able to find one's belongings and having them in good repair, allows a person to move gracefully through the day. This can free up more time to spend having a rewarding life.

If taken too far, however, the ascetics of order and cleanliness causes its own problems. If taken to an extreme and unrealistic level, the quest for a clean and orderly home can become a form of enslavement. In such cases, it interferes with rather than enhances living a rewarding life, leaving no time for creative and meaningful pursuits.

Not surprisingly, the optimal level of order and cleanliness needed for living well varies from person to person. Artists and musicians know the importance of having their tools and instruments ready at hand when the muse strikes, even if this results in cluttering their living space.

Possibilities
- What do you like about the way you have set up or organized your current living space?
- Are there things that you could change at home to enhance your daily life?

Your response to the above questions may not necessarily be about organization. It may have more to do with improving the quality of everyday life in other ways as it was for Ron.

Ron complained:

> I spend several minutes every morning looking for matching socks, belts, and shirts in my closet. I wake up wanting a cup of coffee, and I get so frustrated when ten minutes pass and I'm still in the closet trying to get dressed! It puts me in a foul mood every morning.

Asked what would be the first and smallest sign that things were getting better, he answered:

> I'd give myself a cup of coffee first thing in the morning and take it back into the closet with me. It would be a lot less frustrating if I was drinking that first cup of coffee while I was searching for things. I need to put a little shelf up in the corner of my closet so I have a place to set that coffee cup while I'm pulling out things to wear.

Asked about further signs that things would be getting better or more enjoyable in his morning ritual, he answered:

> I would be listening to good music on the radio while I was looking for my stuff in the morning.

These details could make a difference in the quality of Ron's living space. At no point was he interested in cleaning or reorganizing his closet! It didn't fit for him, and it was not something he would do.

These details could make a difference in the quality of Ron's living space. At no point was he interested in cleaning or reorganizing his closet! It didn't fit for him, and it was not something he would do.

Possibilities
- What do you like about the way you approach each day in your living space?
- Are there things that you would like to change in some way? If so, what would be the result of that difference?
- What would be one small step toward enacting that change?

Designing with Furniture

Don't be afraid to be unconventional in arranging your home. One winter, my sister Lisa moved her living room couch into the kitchen because it was the coziest place in the house to sit while she enjoyed time with her young daughter. Eccentric furniture arrangements and unusual decorating touches are a form of joyous self-expression that can reinvent a living environment while enlivening its inhabitants.

Possibilities
- Do you prefer to sit on chairs, couches, or pillows?
- When choosing furniture, do dramatic, primitive shapes appeal to you, or do you prefer more traditional designs?
- Perhaps you enjoy the detail of ornate wood carvings, or maybe just the opposite. Maybe you like the streamlined effect of clean, modern decor?
- Or do you like an absence of furniture, preferring a few large pillows or a luxurious rug to couches and chairs?

The Ancient Perspective of Feng Shui

When exploring new ideas for arranging your home and your furniture you might enjoy incorporating Feng Shui teachings. An ancient Chinese philosophy about the relationships between humans and their environment, Feng Shui was developed over five thousand years ago. The purpose of this practice is to improve the quality of life by creating environments that are in harmony with nature.

Feng Shui (pronounced "phong shway") practitioners believe that modifying the layout and orientation of homes and workplaces can enhance the well being of the people who inhabit those spaces. Increasingly popular in the West, books on Feng Shui are readily available in most bookstores and libraries. *The Complete Illustrated Guide to Feng Shui: How to Apply the Secrets of Chinese Wisdom for Health, Wealth and Happiness* by Lillian Too is a good introduction.

CHALLENGING THE PROSPERITY MIND-SET

What do you associate with prosperity? I ask this question because people often tell me wistfully that life in their home would be much better if only they were "rich," or if only they had more money than they do now. My sister Margaret, a counselor, likes to ask people how their life would be different if they won the state lottery.

While some people respond to the lottery question with descriptions of things that only additional money could buy, most people also list things that are not dependent on acquiring more money. Once identified, at least some of the things you associates with prosperity may well be within reach.

Possibilities
- What things do you associate with a pleasing, prosperous life?
- What aspects of these things are more associated with behavior or personal style than with money?
- Which are more dependent on money?
- Can you give some of these things to yourself now?
- How might you use your personal creativity to facilitate this?
- What would be the first small step?

Roger told me that the things he associated with "living the good life" included driving an expensive sports car, fresh flowers on the dining room table, real butter in the refrigerator, and drinking a glass of wine with dinner. While he could not afford the expensive sports car, with a bit of planning he could grow the flowers he loved in the garden outside his kitchen door, keep a small package of butter in the refrigerator, and enjoy a glass of wine with dinner.

Tanya associates prosperity with velvety textures, dark carved woods, and silver candlesticks, all seemingly out of reach on her current graduate student budget. How-ever, in the course of attending garage sales and visiting flea markets, she has acquired an assortment of aristocratic looking old chairs (secondhand reproductions) and an elegant but very worn dark wood daybed that she has draped with velvet remnants from discount fabric stores.

Because it had numerous dents, pockmarks, and scratches, she also obtained a dra-matic silver candelabra for almost nothing at an estate sale. Tanya spent a rainy afternoon cleaning and polishing the candelabra with old rags and a toothbrush while watching a favorite vintage movie. It now shines brightly, the nicks and cracks only adding to its patina. Several friends have asked her if it is a family heirloom!

While these objects are not precisely the things Tanya would choose for her dream house if money were no object, they are nonetheless beautiful and afford her a feeling of prosperity. Although she looks forward to refinishing and reupholstering these objects or even replacing them in the future, she is enjoying her home furnishings now.

Possibilities

- Does your living space already reflect your preferences?
- What would be one simple and pleasing way to introduce or add some aspect of those things that bring joy into your home environment?

Fortunately, creativity and flexibility can help here. Creating a living space that reflects your preferences and therefore your Authentic Self can be but need *not* be a financially costly project.

The Greek god of joy, Dionysius, was said to curse people with madness if they refused to honor him by participating in joyous rites. I have wondered at times if per-haps this metaphorical madness was intended not as a punishment, but as a means of release from rigid and preconceived patterns and ideas about life and lifestyles in order to reclaim the ability to be happy. Beware of all-or-nothing thinking when designing tranquillity and beauty into your home. Rigid thinking patterns can cheat you out of the daily pleasure that is rightfully yours.

Sandy loves firelight and frequently laments the fact that she doesn't have a fireplace. Her best friend, Karen, also longs for a fireplace, but she's done the next best thing. Every night Karen sits for an hour listening to beautiful music while enjoying the golden light, flickering flames, and psychological warmth of a half dozen well-placed votive candles.

This chapter has offered a variety of ideas for enhancing your everyday enjoyment of life at home. I encourage you to develop your own adaptations, one small step at a time. Taking positive action to improve the quality of everyday life for yourself and those around you is an immediate aspect of the larger task we all share: creating a place where people feel cared for and in harmony with one another and the world around them. The next chapter focuses on the related task of creating a nurturing environment at your place of work.

CHAPTER THREE

ENJOYING YOURSELF
MORE AT WORK

How Sunday into Monday melts!

—Ogden Nash

As we reach the millennium, people are spending more and more time at work. As a result there is increasing pressure to create work environments that enhance rather than detract from the quality of people's life experiences. The four sections in this chapter offer a variety of ways for you to make work a nurturing and life-enhancing experience. The first section offers numerous suggestions for bringing playfulness and a sense of calm to work as you need them. The next section provides supportive ideas for improving the emotional health of your work place. The last two sections discuss your feelings about work—what you want from work and how you can approach each day with a positive outlook.

ENLIVENING YOUR WORK SPACE

Do you work at home, in an office, in a cubicle, or somewhere else? Do you have a physical space to call your own? If you have a specific area such as an office or a desk to call your own, how does this work space reflect your passions in life?

David was in charge of supervising my work many years ago at a small, rural mental health clinic. I still remember the pleasure of walking into his small office on the Wednesday afternoons when I met with him.

Although situated in a dreary corner of a sterile hospital building surrounded by flat, treeless farmland, the interior of his office evoked the place he would rather be living: the Pacific Northwest. The walls of his office were decorated with large, colorful posters depicting the lush green fern forests and windswept beaches of the Oregon coastline.

At the far end of that same long, ugly institutional corridor where David worked, I shared a tiny windowless basement office with two women colleagues. One neurotic neatnik nonsmoker (me) and two smokers with idiosyncratic filing systems occupied an inadequate space in a clinic with a history of political tension: we were prime candidates for conflict with one another.

Nevertheless, we got along well. We managed to create a friendly environment within the impossibly small physical space we shared. We accomplished this partly through courtesy and partly by hanging brightly colored fabric prints on all the walls. A shared secret enhanced our sense of allied camaraderie.

Behind our office door, and visible only to us, was a life-size poster of the gentleman of our dreams (Clark Gable) wearing an elegant tuxedo and beckoning us to the party of a lifetime. The contrast between the elegant world of Clark Gable and the one we inhabited in that nearly airless office was so vast that it was impossible to see the poster without laughing! Even years later as I write this, I find myself smiling. It reminds me of the value of bringing a sense of humor and playfulness to work.

Possibilities
- Does your work space reflect your personality, nurture your body and mind, and provide creative inspiration for you to do your best work?
- What would be a small and easy thing you could incorporate into your work environment to further enhance your physical or psychological comfort?

A Sense of Play at Work
Once a day and more often on difficult days, Alice opens her file drawer and gently strokes the fur of the teddy bear she bought several years ago as a gift for her nephew. It never made it out of her office. It's not that Alice doesn't like her nephew. She's bought him other teddy bears and many other toys as well.

But Alice decided long ago that she's not going to part with this bear, the soft brown furry one she keeps discreetly in her file drawer. Why? Because something about that cuddly stuffed toy calms her nerves and soothes her when the demands of her job as a busy corporate executive approach an overwhelming level.

Lisa, the receptionist for a woman's health care clinic, openly displays her collection of tiny stuffed animal toys on her desk. She not only has her employers' permission to do this, they encourage it. The toys' cuddly bodies and comical faces bring a smile to people entering the office.

Charlie keeps three small beanbag balls near his desk so that he can take a juggling break now and then. The bags are shaped like little televisions. He states that playing with them clears his mind and he concentrates better afterward.

A talented advertising copywriter, Brad makes good use of his shark hand puppet as a way to get past writing blocks. He says the puppet reminds him of some of his aggressive competitors in the business world. Much to the amusement of his coworkers, when things get stressful in the office and he's having trouble writing, Brad "consults" with the shark, giving it a voice and a humorous perspective. Afterward, he finds he can write again.

Possibilities
- Do you have any toys in your office?
- If not, what might you enjoy?

Things that comforted or amused you as a child can provide clues, but it might be more fun to take a field trip to a local toy store. Anything that makes you laugh is a likely candidate.

If your boss or coworkers are unlikely to appreciate your toy, you can store it discreetly like Alice. However, adding a playful note to an office environment will most likely bring an appreciative smile to your coworkers and visitors.

Living Things Bring Life to Work

My dentist has a beautiful aquarium built into a wall in his reception area. Double-sided, it allows both staff and patients to enjoy the soothing colors and movement of the tropical fish as they glide through the sparkling clean water. I imagine it relaxes the people who work there as much as it does me.

As a psychotherapist, my office waiting area has been enhanced over the years by a series of well-behaved dogs and cats. My clients tell me they find the animals' presence comforting, and some people find it easier to talk while stroking a friendly furry body.

While some offices have rules against animals, their comforting presence can be felt with photos or paintings of animals.

If you have adequate light, a well-tended plant brings a bit of the outdoors inside. Personally I cannot resist the appeal of having at least one real flower on my desk during the summer, and a blooming plant during the cold months.

If your office doesn't boast adequate natural light, a silk plant may provide the same feeling with minimal upkeep. Some people prefer the convenience and long-lasting quality of silk rather than real flowers as a way to have a beautiful bouquet every day.

Possibilities
- How can you best evoke the aspects of nature in your own work place?
- What would be the easiest way to do this?

Your Loved Ones at Work
Lauren brings her two-year-old son to work. Well, not literally. She brings him to work through an ever changing collection of photographs. Her desk also sports photos of her husband, parents, best friend, and the teacher who has always encouraged her. Just looking at the little gallery of smiling faces helps her believe in herself. This is particularly valuable on days when the larger work environment is not as friendly and supportive as she would like.

Possibilities
- What people would you like to be reminded of at work?

Their photographs will generate the same good feelings you experience in their presence. And if you wish to discourage unwanted romantic advances, a prominently placed photo of a spouse or fiancé is a discreet way to communicate that you are in a committed relationship.

Food (and Beverages) for Thought

Erin keeps a supply of her favorite sparkling bottled water in the office refrigerator. In her previous job there was no refrigerator, so she obliged herself with a small cooler for cold drinks. She says having the water on hand prevents her from overindulging in coffee and sodas. Herbal teas are another healthful way to calm the mind and soothe the spirit, and the tea bags take up very little space.

Matthew swears by trail mix, a mixture of seeds, nuts, raisins, and dried fruit that he buys at a local health food store. Allison always keeps granola or a piece of fresh fruit on her desk for the energy burst she knows she will need when things get hectic in the afternoon. Her best friend, Susan, keeps instant noodle soups on hand.

Possibilities
 • What healthful foods or beverages would enhance your workday?

Other Comforts

Do you use the telephone a lot at work? Richard found that spending hours on the phone was literally creating a pain in his neck until he purchased a headphone attachment. Available at telephone supply stores and office supply outlets, headphones also offer the advantage of leaving both hands free to facilitate note taking and doing other work during those times we all spend waiting on hold.

Maureen has a collection of beautiful silk pillows piled in the corner of her office. Reflecting her favorite colors, she takes pleasure in their luxurious texture as well. The pillows also lend a softening effect to the otherwise sterile office environment and provide helpful cushioning for her back muscles when she places one pillow low against the back of her chair.

An early riser, George gets to the office most mornings before it is officially open and the heat is turned on. It is almost always freezing at that early hour. His daughter made him a knitted lap warmer that he uses until the place warms up.

Possibilities
 • What special comforts could you add to your own office?

When Home Is Also Where You Work

Not everyone works in an office outside of their home. Lisa, a computer specialist, does most of her work in a small home office. Since she has a space designated just for work, her ritual is simply leaving the room for the day and closing the door.

My office is at home, a cozy book-lined study overlooking a mountain meadow. The furniture is simple and spare and except for books and a small collection of framed photographs, the walls are bare. The real decoration is the tree-studded landscape outside. I know I have decorated successfully for me because I enjoy working there.

But what if your work space also serves another function within your home such as a dining room or sleeping room? How do you transform your space to accommodate both functions without diminishing the effectiveness and aesthetic quality of the space? After all, you probably don't want to be thinking about work while you're eating dinner or trying to go to sleep. Or maybe you do.

Artists, writers, and musicians sometimes get their best ideas and inspirations while going about the domestic activities of everyday life in the same place that they work. The challenge is to create a physical space that accommodates the necessity of moving from work to rest or play, and vice versa. If physical space is very limited, creating psychological rituals can mark your transition from work to play and relaxation activities.

Living and painting in a studio apartment, Brad substituted rituals for walls to designate his transitions from work to recreation. Rising at dawn, he carries his breakfast out on his tiny balcony to watch the sun come up as he sips his strong black coffee. This is his breakfast room because he keeps his painting supplies on the kitchen table. He marks the passage from work to relaxation by turning off the light over his kitchen table, lighting a beautiful candle, and concentrating on his breathing for a few moments.

Ann, a musician who gives lessons in her living room, marks the end of work by taking a shower and putting on more casual clothes.

Tony, a physical therapist, sees patients in his home gym where he has a massage table. At the end of the day, he burns some sage incense so the room will smell clean and fresh when he uses it to exercise the next morning.

Possibilities
- If you work at home, have you designated areas for business and recreation?
- How do you mark the transition from work to play?

The Traveling Workplace

Sometimes both our work environment and living environment are by necessity a hotel room. Due to my lecture schedule, I spend several nights a month in hotel rooms far from home. Since I love to sew, I always bring a quilt to work on, a heating coil for making tea, tea bags, a small votive candle, and a bar of my favorite jojoba-scented soap. These things fit easily inside a small carry-on bag. The quilt helps transform an unfamiliar room into a place of warmth and comfort.

Whenever possible I purchase fresh local fruit for a quiet breakfast in my room. The details of familiar scents of soap and tea from home, the glow of a candle in the evening, and a piece of beautiful fruit help convert strange hotel rooms into welcoming spaces.

What would help you transform a hotel room into a haven that nurtures your creativity and supports your ability to focus on the work you must do there? Consistency can help, adding a note of relaxing familiarity to an otherwise strange environment. If you prefer a certain kind of pen or other writing implement, it is a good idea to use the same kind wherever you are. The same is true of paper and other office supplies.

You may have no specific office or studio or even hotel room in which you routinely work. Your work may entail constantly moving from one location to another. Fortunately, a work space of your own can be portable.

As a constantly traveling journalist Ed has worked, eaten, and slept in tents, trains, buses, and boats as well as occasional hotel rooms. More than anything else, Ed thinks of his Filofax notebook as his workplace. Compact and portable, it is an external symbol of the very personal work environment that he carries with him everywhere.

Besides serving as his appointment book, the notebook contains maps; airline, train, and bus schedules; plastic pockets for credit cards and for pictures of family, friends and pets; phone numbers; vital work information; and a supply of blank paper.

His notebook also contains clippings of inspiring quotations from some of his favorite writers. Serving as a familiar touchstone, the act of opening the notebook helps

Ed focus his thoughts and make sense of the story developing around him amid the distractions of foreign or chaotic environments.

Possibilities
- What is one small unobtrusive thing you could easily carry—inside a brief-case or book—that would remind you of something that delights you and nurtures your spirit?

Changing the Emotional Atmosphere at Work

While it only takes one person to create conflict or tension in a work relationship, it usually takes two people to maintain it.

Patricia worked as a nurses' assistant in a large hospital. Her work required her to pick up several prescriptions each day from the hospital pharmacy. The hospital pharmacist was a rude older man who seemed to take an instant dislike to Patricia.

Even though the prescriptions were called into the pharmacy several hours before she went to pick them up, the pharmacist never bothered to fill them until Patricia arrived. Even then he often kept her waiting while he filled orders for other people who came after her. He seemed to deliberately ignore her.

Since she had many other duties in addition to picking up the prescriptions, Patricia resented the time she wasted needlessly waiting in line at the pharmacy. When she tried to talk to the pharmacist about filling her prescriptions ahead of time, he always rebuffed her telling her angrily that he was overworked and doing the best he could.

As the months went by, Patricia found herself staying later and later at work, trying to get everything done before she left for the day. She knew that one of the reasons she had to stay late was the time she wasted every day waiting in the pharmacy. Her resentment of the obnoxious pharmacist grew. Thoughts of how much she disliked him began to intrude into her hours away from work. He was ruining the job she had worked so hard to obtain.

Patricia often talked to her mother on the phone and told her about all the misery the horrible old pharmacist was causing her at work. She also told her mother about the kindly old janitor who worked on the same floor as the pharmacy. The janitor always had a friendly word for everyone. Thankfully Patricia saw the janitor when she came out of the pharmacy each day. They liked to tell each other jokes; he cheered her up.

When her mother came for a visit that year, Patricia took off a week from work. Toward the end of her stay, her mother ran out of a necessary prescription. Although she dreaded seeing the pharmacist on her vacation, Patricia offered to fill the prescription at the hospital. Her mother declined. She wanted to go to the pharmacy herself and get a look at the pharmacist and the janitor her daughter had told her so much about.

The following day, after her mother left, Patricia went back to work. When she walked into the pharmacy, the old man greeted her courteously and told her that her prescriptions were ready. Patricia was so astonished that before she thought about what she was saying, she had thanked him politely and wished him a nice day. The next day the prescriptions were ready and waiting for her, and this time the pharmacist wished *her* a nice day. Patricia was completely mystified by the dramatic change in his behavior.

Patricia telephoned her mother and asked what she had said to the pharmacist. Her mother had told the pharmacist what a wonderful job her daughter, Patricia, said he was doing and how seeing him always brightened her day. She added that after going to the pharmacist, she had passed that rude old janitor in the hall, and she knew just what her daughter meant, he really was an obnoxious man! She had not spoken to him, of course.

The courteous relationship continued between Patricia and the pharmacist until he retired five years later.

While replicating Patricia's mother's accidental intervention is unlikely, perhaps you could do something else that would improve the psychological environment between yourself and your coworkers.

Peter works in a public agency fraught with political tension. His position as a liaison between various departments is funded by the federal government. His colleagues, however, must compete with each other for the ever decreasing state and county fund for their programs. This contributes to an emotional climate of distrust and hostility. As the one person whose job is not at risk because of statewide financial cutbacks, Peter would be a natural scapegoat for his colleagues. But he is not.

Several years ago, when he noticed tension building among his colleagues at work, Peter decided to do something to raise morale. He went home after work and spent most of one evening baking several dozen blueberry muffins. He brought them in the next morning and distributed them to each department without a word. Everyone wanted to know where the muffins had come from, but Peter refused to answer. He just smiled and said, "It's a mystery."

That afternoon several people who had not spoken to him for several months greeted him in the hallway. People from various departments began talking to each other, although initially it was just about where the muffins might have come from.

Every few months Peter privately decrees it "mystery muffin day," and brings muffins or other treats to work with no explanation. There has been speculation about who made the muffins, and some people suspect Peter but no one knows for sure. Meanwhile, morale among the agency staff members and relationships between the various departments has continued to improve.

Of course baking muffins can be laborious after a full day of work, and many people don't have the time. Ellen works in a large inner-city insurance office. The building is old, and the fluorescent lights cast a sickly glow on the ugly brown carpet and worn leather furniture. In spring and summer she brings weekly bouquets from her garden.

Ellen gives one bouquet to the receptionist at the front desk that everyone passes when entering or leaving the building. She places another bouquet on her own desk. People comment on the beauty of the flowers; they stand out brightly against their unlikely surroundings.

After Ellen started bringing the bouquets, a coworker started bringing a surplus of tomatoes from his garden to share with coworkers.

Laughter has been proven to reduce the likelihood of contracting stress-related illnesses, and it can also contribute to reducing overall stress in a work environment. Ron regularly brings jokes and cartoons clipped from newspapers and magazines and posts them on the staff bulletin board at the engineering firm where he works.

One design firm contracts with a professional comedian, not to entertain the staff, but to lead them through gentle improvisational comedy exercises to reduce tension thereby stimulating their mental flexibility and enhancing their creativity.

Possibilities
- Are you affected by tension or conflict in your workplace?
- What is one small thing you might do to improve the emotional climate where you work?

CHANGING YOUR INTERNAL WORK ENVIRONMENT

Are you unhappy at work? If you have already done what you need to do to make your physical environment and the shared emotional environment at work comfortable, it may be time to work on your internal environment.

The Role of Self-Talk

Adam complained that he dreaded going to work. He had been feeling this way ever since his company's expansion had necessitated a move to a large modern building across town. Since the physical surroundings of his office had changed, I assumed there was something that he didn't like about his new work space.

Maybe Adam could add something to his office or his desk that would elicit good feelings. When I suggested this, he told me:

> The environment where I work isn't the problem. It's the environment I have going on inside me. I have to do something about my self-talk.

He explained that he began each day by telling himself, "I don't want to be here." Throughout the day this phrase repeated itself in his mind, and the more he thought about it, the more he resented being at work and the less he accomplished.

Each day he was getting further behind. The days dragged on, each feeling like a seemingly endless expanse of time. When he finally reached the end of a workday, Adam left feeling guilty and tired. He was unable to enjoy the hours of freedom he now had because he knew he would have to return the next morning.

The reason Adam didn't want to be at work was not that he hated his job. It was, he said, "as good as any other job, and if I have to work, this is the kind of work I want to do." The problem was that right now he didn't feel like working, period.

It was summer and he would rather be off on his sailboat, or spending time hiking and going on picnics with his girlfriend, a school teacher who had the summer months free. Who could blame him? The trouble was, like most of us, he needed to keep his job to support himself.

Adam was right about needing to change his internal environment, and altering his self-talk was the first step. He decided to replace "I don't want to be here" with "Well, you're here, idiot. Get to work." But this did not foster the internal environment—a positive state of mind—he was looking for.

When I asked Adam what he would say to a younger person with a similar problem, he replied: "You'll feel better if you get to work."

Asked to consider what difference repeating this self-talk and behaving accordingly (getting to work on returning his phone calls, completing his paperwork) would make for him, Adam answered, "I'd be able to leave at the end of the day not feeling guilty. I'd be able to enjoy my time off."

Adam wrote his new self-talk mantra, "You'll feel better if you get to work," on a piece of paper that he taped to his desk where he alone could see it. It took him about three weeks to eradicate the negative self-talk that had been polluting his internal environment, and afterward he felt much better.

Possibilities
- What sort of self-talk do you experience?
- Would it be helpful to change your self-talk? If so what would be the best message to give yourself during the day?

Creating a Symbol to Center Yourself

Elena's work as a professional mediator requires her to participate in tough negotiation sessions without betraying her emotions. Even when others lose their tempers, she always appears calm and cool at the bargaining table. Typically one of Elena's hands is at her side and the other is resting inside her jacket pocket.

What no one knows is that the hand inside her pocket is touching the seashell she always carries with her. Picked up on a beach many years ago, the seashell is ordinary looking and conveniently small.

Touching the shell brings Elena internal peace and a sense of the immense power and vastness that she experiences at the ocean. This affords her a calmness that helps her focus on the larger goals of her life and prevents her from, in her words, "sweating the small stuff."

Possibilities
- When in your life have you felt most relaxed, calm and centered? Select one experience you would enjoy remembering again in the future.
- What was it about this experience that you found most relaxing and meaningful? Notice what images, thoughts, or words come to mind.

If you have trouble thinking of a symbolic object that you could carry like Elena's seashell, ask yourself where and during what experiences in your life have you felt most centered and at ease. Then draw a picture or choose an object, photograph, or quotation that reminds you of that experience to carry with you into your work environment. Use this symbol to center, calm, and replenish yourself when life becomes stressful or when you simply want to relax.

Relaxation, Yoga, and Meditation
Erica enhances her internal environment by meditating. She posts a Do Not Disturb sign on her office door once a day and meditates. When she closes the door, she also closes out all the tension of the day.

There are many ways to meditate. Erica prefers to repeat a single word, *calm*, over and over until she feels her breathing become even and her neck and shoulders relax into what she calls her meditative response.

Carl finds that he accomplishes the same thing by taking time out to say a prayer. Jean mentally relaxes by imagining her thoughts projected on a blackboard. She envisions that with each breath she erases the blackboard until it is a restful clear surface that leaves her with a calm, soothing feeling in her mind and body.

You may prefer to relax by focusing primarily on the sensations in your body. Liz finds that systematically tensing and then releasing her muscles beginning with her toes and progressing up to the top of her head relaxes her best.

A long-time yoga practitioner, David takes a brief break during the day to go through his yoga stretching exercises.

Possibilities
- Do you have a favorite way to relax at work?
- What would help you enhance your own internal atmosphere at work?

FINDING MEANING IN WORK

There are at least three ways to make going to work a meaningful and rewarding experience. The first is the one that is usually talked about in self-help books: finding a way to get paid for doing what you love. Countless New Age gurus suggest that if people really do what they love, they will be good at it and the money will follow.

Do What You Love

Unfortunately, given the current economy and the fact that some jobs are valued more highly than others, doing only work you love is not always a realistic goal. Doing the work you love may earn money, but it may not be the amount you need to survive and live well. And even if your job already entails doing the work you love, chances are it includes other duties as well. Within each person's chosen profession there are usually aspects of work that are less than enjoyable.

As a school counselor, Dee loves working with children and values having summers free to enjoy her own kids. She does not, however, appreciate the tedious record keeping and test administering that her job entails. To cope, she focuses on the aspects of work that she likes best, and deemphasizes the tasks she likes least.

Thinking of the Big Picture

A second way to enhance the meaning and satisfaction you get from work is Big Picture thinking. Rather than concentrating only on the specifics of the job and constantly evaluating what you like and don't like about what you're required to do at work, Big Picture thinking invites you to examine the positive effects your work has on your life and the lives of others.

For example, Suzanne is an airline ticket agent and is required to be at work before five o'clock most mornings. This causes her to miss out on many evening social events during the week. At the same time, her job has many perks. She gets to travel at a reduced rate, and part of the money she is making will help her send her daughter to college.

On those icy mornings when going to work is a bleak prospect, she transforms the day into a meaningful experience by imagining her daughter graduating from college and contemplating the trip she is planning for the spring.

A Higher Goal

On another level, Suzanne finds meaning in her work by being competent and paying attention to detail, thus enhancing the quality of life for the travelers she interacts with. This brings us to a third way to experience gratification in our work. The meaning of work and its potential rewards take on a very different quality if we look at work as a spiritual opportunity, as an effort dedicated to a larger and higher goal than our own personal well-being.

Many religions and cultures suggest that if you are faced with particularly difficult or distasteful work, it can be made meaningful and therefore more tolerable by offering your efforts up to God. This transcendent way of thinking does not have to be the sole territory of saints, mystics, and spiritual leaders. Ordinary people may also be strengthened by focusing their daily efforts on a higher level.

Some people link the transcendent spiritual meaning of their work to a specific goal such as making the world better for future generations. As a result of his efforts as a civil rights activist, Nelson Mandela was incarcerated and sentenced to do menial physical labor. Yet he found a sense of purpose by performing his daily labors in a dignified manner, believing that his actions added further credibility to the political stance he was imprisoned for espousing. He linked his work to a higher goal, that of winning freedom for people of color in South Africa, now and in the generations to follow.

Not everyone who finds a transcendent meaning in their work is famous like Nelson Mandela. Harold is a county employee whose job is collecting garbage in some of the rougher neighborhoods of Chicago. Despite recent improvement in garbage collecting machinery, Harold's work is smelly, physically exhausting, and often involves tolerating excessively cold as well as hot, humid weather.

Despite this, Harold often goes out of his way to pick up additional items people have left out for collection, doing more than his job description requires. Harold has been working at the same garbage collection job for twenty years, and he has always enjoyed making the extra effort. He gets satisfaction from knowing his efforts make the city a better place to live.

Possibilities
- What helps you find meaning in the work that you do?
- Which of the three ways of finding meaning in work most supports your work goals? Notice what you are already doing that helps you accomplish this, and determine whether there is anything you would add or adjust.

Since most of us must earn a living, why not do whatever you can to make the hours spent at work as pleasant and fulfilling as possible? Take a moment to appreciate what you are already doing to accomplish this, and to review any new ideas that occurred to you in reaction to the various sections in this chapter.

This chapter has offered a variety of ways to enhance your quality of life at work. The next chapter invites you to move beyond the realm of your work environment to explore your hopes and dreams.

PART TWO

CREATING A
JOYOUS FUTURE

CHAPTER FOUR

HOPES AND DREAMS

Undoubtedly, we become what we envisage.

—Claude M. Bristol

This chapter will help you explore the cherished dreams, hopes, and goals that you hold in the deepest recesses of your heart, creating the mind-set necessary to achieve your own unique version of them. You deserve to do all you can to make your heart's desires come true. At the highest level, this is neither selfish nor conflictual with spiritual or religious teachings.

In fact, loving oneself is a necessary condition for loving others and loving the world around you. As I write this, it seems that if ever there was a world in need of love, it is certainly the one we are living in now.

The exercises in this chapter will help you reclaim the ability to identify deeply held hopes and dreams and enhance or restore your ability to believe, in fact to expect, that good things can happen in your future. The first two sections in this chapter will help you explore and develop your goals through writing and artistic expression. The next section offers practical ideas for cultivating an attitude that will deepen your ability to enjoy and appreciate both the life you have now and the one you are in the process of creating. The chapter ends with an exercise that will empower you to identify and cultivate in yourself those valued characteristics and qualities you associate with a special person whose influence you would have liked to have had in your life.

If you have experienced numerous painful events, it may initially be difficult to imagine that a series of good things really could happen to you. Developing a belief that good things can happen to you and a mind-set based on the expectation that they will is important because it allows your unconscious to create the psychological and behavioral conditions necessary to support and enhance the positive changes you desire.

Perhaps you're already well-acquainted with the hopes and dreams you cherish, or maybe at this point you're no longer sure what they are. Maybe some of your goals have changed. Or perhaps you've been so busy coping with your life up until now that you have lost track of or forgotten the dreams that once shined brightly for you. That was what had happened to Kate.

Moments after Kate walked through my office door I found myself feeling protective of her. A lovely young woman with gentle brown eyes and flowing dark hair, she focused her gaze primarily on the floor and spoke haltingly, as if she was used to being constantly interrupted.

Her slightly stooped posture, downcast eyes, and nervous habit of repeatedly twisting strands of her hair suggested that Kate had been through a lot in her thirty-odd years and that she was feeling quite disheartened. This turned out to be true.

Sexually and physically abused as a child, rejected and blamed by the parents who should have protected her, Kate had endured a painful childhood. Then as a young adult she had suffered through an excruciating divorce, cruelly betrayed by the man she had loved.

Now a single mother, stuck in a job with an exploitive and obnoxious boss, she felt despairing of her life ever getting better. The only ray of sunshine in her world was her daughter, Tamara. Thanks to Kate's mothering, Tamara was experiencing the once-in-a-lifetime kind of magic and wonder that comes with being five years old in a loving home.

When I asked Kate how she would know that things were getting better in her life, she said: "I don't know. I feel completely overwhelmed. I don't even know what I want anymore. I can't even imagine it getting better. But its got to. I can't go on like this."

Despite her joy in Tamara, other aspects of Kate's life were so miserable that she had contemplated suicide more than once. Fortunately her concerns about the hurtful effects this would have on five-year-old Tamara had prevented Kate from hurting herself.

I say fortunately not only because her daughter needed her, but also because Kate's life would improve significantly, far better than she could imagine the day we first met. If she had killed herself she would not have discovered the bright future awaiting her.

Besides, the world needs people like Kate. She is a kind and good person, a creative and sensitive soul who has a lot to give to other people and to herself. One of the saddest phenomena I have had to face as a psychotherapist is the frequency with which kind, smart, sensitive people like Kate are wounded by life's cruelties.

Despair sometimes prevents people like Kate from taking the actions needed to finally get the life they deserve, a life that would heal the pain they've been through and help them experience the joy of being alive.

If you've been through a series of painful life experiences, you too may occasionally feel hopeless. But don't be trapped into believing that you are going to feel that way for the rest of your life. Even though life can seem overwhelming and impossible, feelings do change. And you can take steps, one at a time, to move your life in the direction you want.

A first step is to figure out what you want and to believe that it's possible to attain that goal. The following Letter from the Future exercise will help you rediscover your unique hopes and dreams, and reclaim a way of thinking that was stolen from many of us in childhood through trauma or abuse or even the educational process that often ridicules or even punishes daydreaming. The following exercise, based on creative imagining, is among the most powerful of the exercises in this book.

A LETTER FROM THE FUTURE

This imaginative process is often relegated to the exclusive terrain of inventors, writers, artists, musicians, and creative geniuses, but is actually an inborn human ability that belongs to all of us. When we lose our ability to dream, we lose a lot of our potential for joy. Most of us could benefit from occasionally taking time to reclaim and strengthen this natural gift.

 One Small Step
Pick a time in the future (five, ten, fifteen, twenty years from now or any other length of time that is meaningful to you). Record the future date you have chosen at the head of your letter. Imagine that the intervening years have passed and you are writing to a friend. Choose someone you know and with whom you would like to continue to be friends in the future. Use the friend's name in the salutation, as in Dear (friend's name).

When writing the letter, imagine that you are living a joyous, healthy, satisfying life by the letter's date. If there are problems with which you are now struggling, assume that they have either been resolved or that you have found satisfying ways to cope with them by the time of the letter.

Explain how you resolved problems or difficulties that once plagued you. Tell what you found to be most helpful from the vantage point of looking back on your current life from the future.

Describe in detail how you spend your time in this imaginary future. What is a typical day? Where are you living? Describe your relationships, beliefs, reflections on the past, and speculations toward the more distant future.

This letter is not meant to be mailed. It is for you only. The purpose of dating the letter and writing it to a real person is to strengthen the psychological realism of the letter for you on both conscious and unconscious levels.

Here is a small portion of the letter that Kate wrote:

January 27, 2010

Dear Sarah,

Here is the letter I promised to write after Christmas.

This year has passed so quickly that I have not had time to write very often. I hope this finds you well. I have been enjoying my work ever since I left my old job. I wake up each morning in a great mood. I have been able to maintain the weight I took off at Weight Watchers.

On a typical day, I get up early, do a few exercises, and wake up Tamara in a good mood. Then I drop her off at school and go to work. At night I either relax with Tamara, go out with a friend, or do something creative. I am dating a very nice man. Tamara continues to be a great joy in my life. Life is good these days, and I feel lucky to be alive.

In writing your letter, don't worry about limiting yourself to things that seem realistic given your current life. This is not essential and may constrict you unnecessarily. Your Letter from the Future should be written with an open heart and an open mind so you have room to surprise yourself.

John, for example, had lived in a flat landlocked area of the Midwest all his life. He was very surprised when he described himself in his Letter from the Future as living on the coast of Hawaii. Although this did not seem readily achievable when John was writing his Letter from the Future, he allowed himself to write about it anyway.

Writing his letter eventually led to some important discoveries about who he was, what he loved most, and how he could create more joy for himself. As a result, John had some remarkable adventures that he could not have anticipated before writing his letter. He participated in a teacher's exchange program that allowed him to spend a year teaching in Papau, New Guinea. Later he spent a summer vacation backpacking through Japan. His visit to a Japanese Zen monastery was the beginning of a continuing interest in Buddhist principles and philosophy. Years later, the experiences and discoveries that emerged as a result of his Letter from the Future continue to inspire him.

If for some reason you don't enjoy writing, you might dictate your Letter from the Future into a tape recorder or mentally record it. However, I have found over the years that this exercise tends to be most powerful when actually written. The psychological realism created by writing and dating an actual letter lend to the exercise's impact. Take some time now before going further in this chapter to write your own Letter from the Future.

Possibilities
- Now that you have completed your letter, what did you learn?
- What did you include in the letter that is not yet happening in your life?
- What do you imagine would be the result of this happening?
- What is a first step you might take toward your desired future?

Keep this letter in some safe and private place where you can refer to it as needed. After writing her letter, Kate told me:

> It's only an imaginary letter, but I find myself feeling more hopeful. The letter seemed to give me the idea that things could get better. And after I wrote it, I realized that there were a couple things in it that I could do now, even before I get a new job.

Kate's letter may appear to be more down-to-earth than John's, but the changes it eventually led to in her life were just as large.

As is usually the case, the immediate results of Kate's letter were small and gradual. She had a good week after writing her Letter from the Future. Her face brightened as she explained to me that using her letter for guidance, she had started her workday mornings more playfully with Tamara much like she had envisioned in the letter, and she had hired a baby-sitter so that she could have dinner with a friend the following week.

But there was still a sadness in her eyes, and her shoulders seemed weighed down, as if she were still carrying the burden of some of the bad things that had happened in her past. After a moment of quiet reflection she blurted out:

> I'm scared. Things feel a little bit better, but I'm afraid I'm going to lose sight of what I wrote about in the letter and it will all fall by the wayside, and I'll always be stuck in this job. I've tried to change before and it never seems to work. I don't carry through. I intend to, but I don't.

Kate had a good point. She had a right to be afraid. Change is hard, and it is all too easy to live a life based primarily on our fears rather than pursuing heartfelt hopes and dreams. What Kate needed now was a way to counterbalance the bad things that had happened in the past that were weighing her down. Otherwise she was in danger of losing sight of the different kind of future she was beginning to formulate in her mind.

Kate needed something that would make her new future even more vivid, so brilliant that it would be impossible to forget. She needed something tangible to hang onto to keep her dreams and goals that gave her hope and strength prominent in her thinking. Her next assignment, a Heart's Desire Collage, would serve this purpose.

THE HEART'S DESIRE COLLAGE

The Heart's Desire Collage will amplify the hopes and dreams you described in your Letter from the Future. Giving them a tangible representation will also strengthen their presence in your unconscious.

Collect symbolic items ahead of time by assembling some photos, postcards, drawings, or images from magazines that remind you of your heart's desires. Pieces of paper, leather, or fabric in your favorite colors are also appropriate because they can evoke the positive feelings you associate with various shades and textures. You may also want to include objects from nature such as twigs, dried flowers, or small shells. Don't forget any work you have drawn yourself.

You can also write words directly on your collage. For example, when Kate made her Heart's Desire Collage, she added the words, "I deserve good things to happen. I deserve happiness."

 One Small Step
Set aside at least an hour for this exercise. Where you spend this time is important. Make sure you have privacy or, if there are people around, they should be nonjudgmental and supportive of what you are doing. You will need a piece of cardboard or heavy paper at least 8 by 10 inches, scissors, glue, writing or drawing tools, and a collection of things that symbolize the hopes and dreams you began to explore in your Letter from the Future.

Now glue your collected objects onto the piece of cardboard or paper. Arrange things in any pattern that pleases you. You can overlap or layer items, create a picture, or randomly paste things into a design that abstractly expresses your heart's desire for your future.

Take a moment to note what you have learned and how you feel.

 Possibilities
• What was it like to create a collage based on your hopes and dreams?
• What were you thinking about as you made your Heart's Desire Collage?
• Stop and look at it. What does it tell you about who you are deep inside, beyond life's irritations, distractions, and pain?

When making your collage, remember that the goal is to rediscover the free and childlike imagination of your Authentic Self. That means you are allowed to be playful and spontaneous, and it's fine to be messy. Don't be surprised if additional ideas occur to you while you're in the middle of making the collage. This is common.

Store your Heart's Desire Collage in a place where you will see it regularly, perhaps in a drawer where you keep belongings you use every day. (I kept mine in my sock drawer for several years.)

If you are a typical westerner, your Heart's Desire Collage probably included a number of possessions you would like to have in the future. Kate's did. Along with a picture of a woman sitting at a desk looking happy (to represent feeling good at work), snapshots of herself and her daughter, and heart cutouts symbolizing a future love relationship, she also included a clipping of some wonderful white wicker furniture that she longed to have on her enclosed porch and an image of a beautiful new car she had cut out from an advertising brochure.

There is nothing wrong with including material items in your Heart's Desire Collage. In fact doing so often indicates that you are making progress toward allowing yourself to feel deserving of the material things you want. It is a sign that you have moved beyond the negative mind-set that is typically created by experiencing painful life events. It is good to get what you want.

YOUR HAPPINESS

The next chapter in this book is dedicated to helping you move toward your goals. However, before we move beyond discovering *what* you want into the specifics of how to make it happen, we need to talk about happiness.

We've all heard the phrase, "Money won't make you happy." While I've heard that said over and over, I've heard the rejoinder just as often: "I'd like to be in the position to find out!" Most people associate possessing certain material belongings with happiness.

According to extensive research at the University of Chicago—excluding situations of abject poverty in which people do not have adequate food, shelter, and clothing to survive—there is no correlation between material wealth and happiness (Csikszentmihalyi, 1990).

The best and most succinct way of stating the relationship between one's heart's desires—material and otherwise—and happiness that I have found is something I once read on an antique sampler:

It's not how much we have, but how much we enjoy that brings happiness.

Enjoyment is an ability that can be learned and once learned, expanded. The final section of this chapter offers two exercises designed to enhance your capacity to enjoy the life that you are in the process of creating.

Cultivating the Gratitude Attitude
In her wonderful book, *Simple Abundance*, Sarah Ban Breathnach suggests that people should keep a daily record of things for which they are grateful in a gratitude diary. This record can be incorporated into your existing journal, or you could devote a special blank book to these entries.

Even if you don't go to the trouble of writing down what you are grateful for each day, asking yourself what you could be grateful for will have an encouraging effect because it shifts your thinking into a positive direction.

One Small Step
Cultivate your own Gratitude Attitude. Identify at least three things for which you could be grateful. Think about these three beneficial things, and then notice what happens to your mood as you do this. Repeat this exercise once a day for the next week, and notice what happens after you identify the three (or more) favorable things in your life. Notice how easy or difficult this is for you, and most important, notice the effect doing this has over accumulated days.

Although it is not true for everyone, Kate found listing things for which she was grateful fairly easy. The image of her beautiful little daughter, her friends, and the fact that she was healthy came to mind immediately. Kate noticed that repeating her Gratitude Attitude list last thing at night helped her relax and feel more peaceful as she drifted off to sleep, and when she did it first thing in the morning, she felt less intimidated by the demands of the day.

Creating a New Influence for Your Life

Children learn by modeling. Later in life our ability to live a satisfying, joyous life is still effected for better or worse by the people who have influenced our thinking and way of living. The significant people in our life and their effects on us happens randomly and without our having much control.

This was certainly true for Kate who observed after a week of making her nightly gratitude list:

> This is such a good thing to do. I explained it to Tamara, and we have started doing it together as a little game before I put her to bed at night. She loves it. I wish I had had someone in my life to teach me things like this. It may sound terrible but at times I wish I had different parents because mine were not always a very positive influence on me. They didn't put much value on enjoying their lives and their children, and I'm afraid that has had a bad effect on me.

In the following exercise you will consciously choose someone you would like to have had as an influence on your life and to integrate some of their perceived wisdom into your consciousness. This exercise can counterbalance influences that were not always positive or helpful.

 One Small Step

Think of someone who embodies a way of living that you value, a person you admire in some way. This person can be living or dead, famous or unknown. He or she can be someone you know personally or someone you are acquainted with only through literature, movies, or stories you have heard. If at all possible, find a picture of this person (or draw one) to look at while doing this exercise.

Write a detailed description of this person, emphasizing the qualities that you most admire.

Think about why you have chosen him or her to be an influence in your life.

Possibilities
- What do you find most appealing about this person's approach to life?
- How would this person respond to your current situation?

When choosing a person to be a new influence, Kate thought of many people she had admired over the years including her best friend's mother, Alma. But on further reflection, she realized that Alma would not be a new influence. Kate had already enjoyed a close relationship over many years with both Alma and her daughter, which had helped Kate create a loving relationship with her own daughter.

Kate surprised herself by selecting Mr. Stanley, her seventh grade science teacher, as her new influence. She hadn't known him personally, but she had felt very supported and encouraged by him in class. He was one of the few teachers she had in grade school or high school who encouraged girls to consider science as a profession. Kate sensed he had liked and respected her. He had believed in her abilities enough to encourage her to enter a scholarly science competition which she had won.

Sadly, Mr. Stanley was now long dead. With this exercise, however, the qualities Kate associated with him could still become a more prominent influence on her current life. Although she chose him spontaneously and intuitively, Mr. Stanley was a good choice for Kate. He embodied many of the values she needed to embrace before creating the life she needed and wanted. Kate would subsequently place more trust in her own intuition.

Here is a portion of Kate's response to the Creating a New Influence exercise:

Mr. Stanley was a kind person. You could just tell by the way he looked at you from behind those heavy old-fashioned plastic glasses. He was also very smart. I never saw him stumped by a question in class, and yet he was not at all conceited.

If I imagine what Mr. Stanley would say or do in my current situation, I imagine him quietly going about his business, but at the same time being very strong. He wouldn't put up with any nonsense from his students or anyone else, and I'm sure he wouldn't put up with any ridiculous demands from my boss. He would just say no in his very calm, solid way.

He had a way of talking so that when he said something you knew he meant it. Mr. Stanley was also someone who never stopped learning new things. If he were in my situation, he would be using it as an opportunity to learn. He'd be taking all kinds of new training whenever it was available, and eventually that would help him get a better job.

 One Small Step
Think back to the person you chose as a new influence for your life.

Possibilities
- How are you like the person you described in the Creating a New Influence exercise?
- How are you different?
- What aspects of this person's lifestyle do you wish to incorporate into your life?
- Are there any things that you are already doing that are examples of this? If so, what would be the effect of doing a little more of this in order to integrate this quality further into your personality? If not, what would be the first small step toward embodying their way of living?

If you don't believe you possess any of your chosen person's admirable qualities, what would be a small observable sign in your behavior that showed you were beginning to incorporate such qualities? Consider a scale of 1 to 10 in which 10 meant you had succeeded in incorporating a newly desired quality into your behavior to the fullest degree possible, and 1 meant not at all.

What observable practice could you undertake that would raise your score a half point or more? Experiment with enacting the behavior you identified, noticing the difference doing it makes for you. Then identify the next small step that would develop the desired quality and try that, and so on.

The first step Kate identified was to make a conscious effort to behave in a calm, unruffled way at work as she imagined Mr. Stanley would have done. She soon found herself behaving quietly with strength and self-assurance when around her boss, in a way that reminded her of Mr. Stanley. When she found herself being unfairly pressured by her boss or coworkers, she imagined Mr. Stanley's face.

She told me:

> It's strange but I feel much more respected at work since I created the influence of Mr. Stanley in my life. My boss seems to sense that I am stronger. He hasn't been trying to get me to work after hours anymore. It's almost like I've taken on some "male energy" that helps me stand up for myself at work.

What differences did you experience as you incorporated your chosen influence into your life? In the days and weeks to come, notice how the influence you created shows up in your own life. It may be helpful to imagine the face of your chosen person at difficult and challenging moments.

After beginning the daily Gratitude Attitude ritual and completing the Creating a New Influence exercise, you should feel much stronger and more confident. You may be ready to tackle some of the additional changes in your life you envisioned in your Letter from the Future and your Heart's Desire Collage.

You have been building up your inner strength and self-knowledge as you have progressed through the exercises in this chapter. Before moving on, take a moment to appreciate what you have learned about who you are and what brings you joy.

CHAPTER FIVE

YES, YOU CAN!
TRANSFORMING HOPES AND DREAMS INTO AUTHENTIC REALITIES

Whatever you can do or dream you can, begin it.
Boldness has genius, power and magic in it.

—Goethe

This chapter will help you progress toward living the life you want in the future, teaching you steps that will eventually lead to a "miracle" in your life. One definition of a miracle is "a course correction" (Wapnick, 1989). In defining a personal miracle as a course correction, I do not mean to exclude the spiritual aspect of a miracle, but rather to emphasize personal action as opposed to passive thinking or waiting. As Benjamin Franklin once observed, "God helps those who help themselves."

In the first section of this chapter you will envision a bridge to your desired future. The next section invites you to imagine a miracle, and then identifies the steps needed to create your miracle and keep yourself on track toward your dreams and goals.

A MIRACLE BRIDGE

My early childhood was spent on an isolated rural peninsula of land separated, island-like, from the mainland, reachable only by a thirty-minute ferry ride across the water. On the mainland people could shop at well-stocked grocery stores, acquire needed hardware, buy toys for their children, yarn to knit sweaters, and fabric to sew warm clothing needed for our rugged winters.

Regular boat trips were necessary because these essentials were not obtainable on our little peninsula. As a child it seemed that everything we needed to make our life exciting and happy was available on the mainland.

Far too often the distance between the two peninsulas was insurmountable. Storms and high winds made the crossing so treacherous that the ferries were often canceled. I remember standing in our kitchen and looking out the window at the dark blue-grey water. As I saw the white-capped waves growing larger and larger, I knew that I wouldn't be going on my long-awaited visit to the 5 and 10 cent store on the lower peninsula.

Fortunately, the problem of crossing the water was eventually solved with a bridge—constructed of long metal strands suspended high above the water—spanning the five-mile distance between the two peninsulas. Many residents of our small town had scoffed at the idea that a bridge could be built across two points so far apart. Consequently after the bridge was completed, it was often called the "miracle bridge." The bridge changed life in our town, allowing people to live with greater ease and pleasure than before.

At some junctures, the things we want from life may seem just as unreachable as the mainland did from our small isolated town on stormy days. The exercises in this chapter will empower you to gradually create your own psychological Miracle Bridge to the life you've been wanting, incorporating your hopes, dreams, and goals.

THE MIRACLE QUESTION

Kate (from the last chapter) was feeling better, but she needed an even greater boost to achieve a sense of happiness and personal accomplishment. She needed a bridge that would span the gap between the life she wanted and the constrictions of the life she had.

I really like what I described in my Letter from the Future and what I put into my Heart's Desire Collage, but it's hard for me to imagine exactly how I could make any of the bigger things in them happen, like getting a new job. Sometimes I feel it would take a miracle to change the life I'm actually living into the life I really want.

The Miracle Question (invented by Steve de Shazer and Insoo Kim Berg) is the first step to building a bridge to your desired future. It asks you to imagine and describe what a miracle in your life would look like.

One Small Step

Imagine that in the middle of the night, while you were asleep, a miracle happened and the problem or problems currently troubling you have either been resolved or you have found a satisfactory way to cope with them. Allow yourself to suspend any doubts, cynicism, or skepticism, and simply notice what comes to mind as you explore the fantasy of this miracle occurring. What would be different?

Since you were asleep when the miracle transpired, when you awakened the next morning you didn't know it had happened. As you went through your day, you began gradually to notice signs that things were different, that the problems you had been struggling with on the previous day were now resolved.

When Kate was asked the Miracle Question, she didn't respond immediately. Then she began with a phrase she had used a lot in previous conversations, "I don't know..."

To some people the words "I don't know" sound merely tentative, a disclaimer of sorts about what will follow. However, people can get in the habit of saying "I don't know" when their thoughts and feelings have been repeatedly discounted by others. This is particularly true when you have experienced a lot of invalidating responses from your parents.

As a psychotherapist I hear something else in those words. "I don't know" can be the magic phrase that allows you to safely dare to imagine things you would not otherwise consider.

Kate finally answered, "I wouldn't be working there anymore, period. And I wouldn't be getting up in the middle of the night worrying about the future."

Like most people, Kate's initial response to the Miracle Question was to identify what she *wouldn't* be doing after a miracle changed her life. As she struggled to further develop her imaginary miracle, I invited her to envision what new things she *would* be doing. After puzzling over this for a few moments, she thought of several ideas:

> I would look forward to going to work. I would always be back home at 5:30 in the afternoon.

I would play with Tamara when I got home because I wouldn't be so tired. Or if she was coloring I might clean up our house so it wasn't so depressing to look at. Actually if a miracle happened, my house would already be clean and I would love the way it looked inside.

I would have time to do creative things like painting watercolors or picking up my pen and playing with some lettering like I used to do.

And I would have lost weight. I would be slim and fit.

If you haven't already done so, take some time now to answer your Miracle Question. If you find it freeing to start with a disclaimer, you can begin with "I don't know" and then continue your description. Remember to focus on the specifics of what *would* be happening rather than what *wouldn't* be happening after your miracle has occurred.

Small Signs of a Miracle

The next step is to figure out the first signs that would indicate your miracle has happened. These details are the planks necessary to constructing your Miracle Bridge.

Possibilities
- What would be the first small observable sign that would tell you your miracle had occurred and things were different?
- What would others notice in your behavior that would first indicate that a miracle had happened in your life?
- What would the people who live with you notice?
- What would the people who work with you notice?

If you have trouble coming up with small signs that your miracle has happened, try this: Imagine that you have a videotape of yourself that started running the moment your miracle happened in the middle of the night. What would you notice yourself doing if you were watching the videotape of yourself the first day (and night) after your miracle had happened? What would be the first image or frame on the videotape that would indicate to you that your miracle had happened? What would be the next one?

It can also be helpful to imagine what a young child would notice since their observations tend to be clear in their simplicity. In the same vein, you might imagine what a pet such as a cat or a dog would notice if they were able to talk and tell you about it!

Remember, we are looking for signs of behavioral changes in your life. These tend to be the most empowering because they are specific things you can choose to do. If they are appropriately small, these changes are ideal for constructing the first strands of your Miracle Bridge.

Beginning with her trademark "I don't know," Kate was soon off and running as she described very specific signs that would attest to her miracle:

> I would wake up in the morning, and I would be in a good mood because I'd have a new job that I like. Since I would be in a good mood, I would probably go into my daughter's room and wake her up in an upbeat kind of way. Maybe I would tickle her or make a joke or something. I'd reach down and give her a little kiss on her forehead. I'm already doing that a little bit more these days. And since I was in a good mood, I would have gotten up early, so I would have time to exercise on my stationary bike. I would ride my bike in front of the TV while Tamara ate her cereal and watched *Sesame Street*. Tamara would be surprised that I was exercising.

Making It Real

To make your miracle a reality you must undertake one of the small behavioral indicators that attest to its having happened. Gradually, you can incorporate additional changes into your life until you have eventually built a bridge to the miracle you envisioned.

 One Small Step

Start small, with one step, working one day at a time, first enacting the easiest behavior that would be a sign your miracle has happened. Don't overwhelm yourself with too much at first; this could intimidate you and jeopardize or sabotage your experience.

Easiest of all might be to begin by considering whether you are already doing something, even rarely, that you listed as a sign of your miracle having happened. What would be the effect of doing this more than you have in the past? If such an action leads in the direction of your miracle then continuing or increasing it will be the first step in building your Miracle Bridge.

People who repeatedly complain about a problem but do nothing about it are often viewed as lazy. But what looks like laziness in unhappy people is usually a fear of failure. Lacking confidence in their abilities, they are overwhelmed with the distance between the life they have now and the life they want. The goal is to help you bridge this distance by reducing it to a series of steps so small and gradual that you are *under*whelmed.

I asked Kate whether in the following week she could get up in the morning and kiss her daughter's forehead and be playful with her, and then ride her stationary bike for a while before leaving the house.

She was clearly heartened and said, "Of course I can do that. It doesn't seem like too much. I'm already doing part of that now with my daughter. Shouldn't I be doing more?" I explained the value of starting small.

Even your smallest changes in behavior can have positive repercussions on those around you. For instance, Kate's daughter, Tamara, responded favorably to her mother being in a good mood and being playful with her in the morning. Tamara's happy response further reenforced Kate's new behavior.

By imagining small, active, observable signs of our personal miracle, we identify achievable and nonintimidating behaviors that we can develop. Because these behavioral changes are modest and specific, you will be able to honor your commitment to doing them—both initially when they are less daunting and over time as they remain undemanding. And as sure as the sun comes up in the morning, these gradual behavioral changes will eventually lead to the bigger changes that complete your unique personalized version of a miracle.

If the steps you identify seem needlessly small, you can always extend them, taking care to make them no larger than is realistic for you to do in the next few days. If a step feels challenging but not intimidating, you are welcome to try it.

The Next Small Steps

When she returned a week later, after setting the goal of incorporating two small signs of a miracle—starting the day in a good mood and riding her stationary bike each morning before work—into her everyday life, Kate told me, "I feel better. Not fabulous, but definitely better. I can't say I love my life, but I dislike it less. Now what?"

Possibilities
• What would be the next small sign that would characterize your miracle?

In Kate's case, she answered without hesitation, "I'd go on a diet."

I worried that going on a diet might be overwhelming in the face of the other life changes she was undertaking. Kate assured me it was not. She understood the need to gradually build a bridge of small signs to her real-life miracle. She planned to break the process of losing weight into a series of small steps. Since she had experienced good results with Weight Watchers several years ago, Kate decided that the first step would be to find out where meetings were held in her area. The next step would be to attend a meeting.

So in the following week Kate attended her first meeting and started on the Weight Watcher's program. She continued to ride her stationary bike. She also continued to wake her daughter up playfully each morning. "It sets the tone between us in a positive way for the rest of the day. We have both been joking more and having a happier time together later in the day when I pick her up from school."

Two weeks later Kate reported that she had lost seven pounds and was feeling a lot less depressed about her job even though she still hated going there. And she had more energy.

In subsequent weeks, Kate began practicing her calligraphy, started going out with a friend once a week, and cleaned and reorganized her house—further signs that her miracle had happened. None of these actions directly related to her problematic job, but were things over which she had more immediate control.

After three months, Kate said to me, "I've got to start sending out resumes so I can get out of this job. It's such an obvious thing to do, I don't know why I didn't feel able to do it before, especially since it's the main thing I dislike about my life." Kate sat straight in her chair, her shoulders no longer stooped.

Mornings on her bike and weekly visits to Weight Watchers had paid off. She had achieved her goal of losing weight. Getting out of the house with a friend for an occasional night out had reduced some of the loneliness and boredom that contributed to her depression. Kate was feeling better. The idea of sending out her resume no longer felt overwhelming. She had the energy to do it now, and she also had the confidence to handle any rejections she might encounter during her job search. Her Miracle Bridge was now big enough and strong enough to support her safely over the rough waters that are part of job interviews.

When Kate's job search took longer than she had expected, she was able to persevere and eventually find a new job where she is treated with respect and fairness. Although finding a companion was not part of her original miracle, she has recently begun to date a kind, sensitive man. The rudimentary aspects of her miracle were in place to sustain her as she constructed the remainder of her bridge to the life she had imagined.

What would be the next small sign that would characterize *your* miracle? Try doing the next active sign you identified at the first available opportunity. Notice what difference it makes. Then pat yourself on the back! You have just completed another link in the bridge to your miracle! This process can be repeated as needed until you have created the changes you desire in your life.

Charting Your Progress
One of the advantages that Kate had in creating her miracle was that in working with me she had a witness for her progress, someone she could use to gauge how she was doing. Although it is possible to create your miracle without this, having someone to recognize your gradual progress will help you stay on track.

If there is a supportive and nonjudgmental person already in your life who would be willing to acknowledge and validate your progress, you could tell them some of the details of your miracle and invite them to witness your small steps toward your miracle.

Unfortunately, supportive and nonjudgmental people are not always readily available when we need them! And even good friends or family members who are otherwise accepting and kindly toward you may inadvertently become threatened by the idea that you are in the process of changing. They may directly or indirectly express well-intentioned skepticism or offer advice that could interfere with the momentum you are building in creating your Miracle Bridge.

If you do not have someone to reflect your progress toward your miracle, you can use the following device instead.

 One Small Step

Start by drawing a line with a mark on each end (substitute any symbol you like for the marks):

Imagine that the mark on the left side indicates where you were on your Miracle Bridge before you answered the Miracle Question. The mark on the right side indicates the point in your future when you are living the marvelous life you imagined in your Letter from the Future, your Heart's Desire Collage, and your Miracle Question.

Now draw a mark at the point on your Miracle Bridge to represent where you currently are.

Take a moment now to make a mark on your own Miracle Bridge to represent where you are now in your progress toward your miracle.

Possibilities
- What do you need to do to move yourself one step further along your Miracle Bridge?
- What small step could you take, or continue, that would acknowledge your progress? Consider actions that could be completed in the next few days.

For example, at this point in her life, Kate has already accomplished many things that are part of the life she desires, but there are other changes that would bring additional meaning and joy to her life. She would position herself on her Miracle Bridge here:

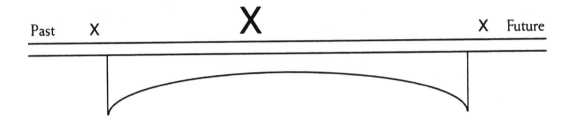

Refer back to your Miracle Bridge as often as needed in the coming days, weeks, and months as you move through the additional exercises in this book toward creating a life you love. Creating a joyful life is a lifelong journey, and you can use your Miracle Bridge for several years. Or you may prefer to apply the Miracle Bridge to shorter term objectives, and draw a new line for each new goal.

Continue to nurture your dreams by envisioning your miracle life and the realities you imagined earlier in this and the previous chapter. Ask yourself the Miracle Question anytime you are feeling stuck or are despairing about a problem, unable to imagine it resolved. The Miracle Bridge is a tool to bypass the mental roadblocks that prevent you from moving beyond your problems and on to solutions.

The next chapter will focus on how your relationship with time can augment your progress in creating the rewarding and satisfying life you truly deserve.

Chapter Six

Time on Your Hands

Unlike other resources, time cannot be bought or sold,
borrowed or stolen, stocked up or saved, manufactured, reproduced,
or modified. All we can do is make use of it.

—Stephen Rechtschaffen

Most of us spend half of our time wishing for things we could have
if we didn't spend half our time wishing.

—Alexander Woolcott

How have you filled the space between now and when you first opened this book? What has changed in your life? What has remained the same? What is your relationship with time like?

If your answer to the last question was "I never have enough time," or "I have too much time on my hands," you are not alone. Most of us seem to have a rather adversarial relationship with time. There's never enough of it; it sometimes passes without us realizing it; and then some days when we are waiting for it to pass, it feels like there's far too much of it. How can we make time work for us instead of against us? This chapter will tell you just that.

The first section in this chapter will help you ascertain your own wise perspective about time and identify the priorities in your life. The next section offers strategies for getting control of your time, enabling you to spend it in ways you value. The final section invites you to explore the rhythms of your body's natural clock and to experience the benefits of "timelessness."

CHANGING PERSPECTIVES ABOUT TIME AND YOUR LIFE

Recently, on a long cross-Atlantic flight, I was seated next to an attractive woman in her late sixties. As we chatted I was struck by the serene expression on her face and her soft voice with its gentle Spanish accent.

There is something about being awake in the middle of night while flying above a darkened ocean that can encourage conversations between two strangers. A few hours into the flight, as Lilliana and I gazed out the window of the darkened cabin, we both commented with awe on the immensity of space above and below us.

Just as the moon rose from behind the clouds, Lilliana told me she had been recently diagnosed with cancer. This was the second time in her life that she had been diagnosed with this disease. Before I could say anything, she stopped me. "Don't feel sorry for me. The cancer has taught me to make every moment of my life count. Life is a precious gift."

I asked how she was spending her time that made it count for her.

Lilliana paused for a moment before answering:

> It's not so much what I do, it's the *attitude* I do it with. I have these two sweet little dogs. Just enjoying sitting on the patio petting them is one way I make my time count. It's just a little thing, an everyday activity, but you see, I *appreciate* it. Time with my husband, just being with him, doing ordinary things like eating a meal together, holding hands, reading in bed together, listening to the radio. These things make my life good.
>
> I know these things seem like very ordinary things and they are. I used to do these same things when I was younger, before I had cancer for the first time, but it's like I wasn't really having the experience of them. My mind was always a little bit off somewhere else, always preoccupied, thinking of some project or chore or worry. Not now.

Lilliana noticed the tears in my eyes before I could blink them away, and continued:

> I know it's sad to think about dying. It makes me sad to think that someday I'm not going to be around to pick up my baby grandson and cuddle him on

my lap, and smell the spring flowers, and talk to my husband and my daughter and son. But we all die and that's not what's important to me right now. Enjoying being alive is what matters, and that's what I'm doing. Do you understand?

Looking out at the night sky, we talked some more, and after our conversation had drifted to husbands, children, and gardening, Lilliana and I both fell asleep. When I woke a few minutes before the plane landed, I told Lilliana what a gift it had been to talk with her.

I hope Lilliana beats the cancer again. Regardless of whether she wins her battle against the disease, she is already succeeding in valuing and enjoying the experience of being alive, fully using the time she has.

After meeting her, I found myself wanting to live more like the way she described —more soulfully, more in the present, more joyously aware of daily life experiences.

The idea of confronting one's mortality as a way to more fully embracing life is not new. Plato advised, "Practice dying." In *The Teachings of Don Juan*, Carlos Castaneda describes the shamanic view of death as an ever present companion and potential helper. Being consciously aware of the eventuality of death can help you stay focused on your goals and maintain a meaningful perspective toward everyday life.

Practicing Dying

The following exercise will help you shift into your own wise perspective about how to spend the time you still have available in your life. Record your response so that you can refer to it afterward.

 One Small Step

Imagine that you have been told that you have only six months to live. Assume for the purposes of this exercise that although you have an incurable illness, thanks to the miracles of modern medicine you will remain relatively symptom free and able to move around comfortably until the final moments of your life.

Possibilities
- How would you wish to spend the remaining months of your life?
- Who are the people you would want to spend time with?
- What places would you like to visit or revisit?
- Are there any specific things you would need to do to enhance a feeling of completion and peacefulness before you die?

Take a few moments now to examine your responses to the above questions; they hold valuable clues as to how you might best prioritize your time and more fully honor your most heartfelt longings and needs. What is the first small step you could take to incorporate these changes into your daily life? Now embark on this first project. Life is too short to not live it in a genuine way!

When Nancy came to see me for psychotherapy she described herself as being in the middle of a midlife crisis. She was experiencing a pervasive dissatisfaction with her current life and was unsure about what she wanted for the future. Asked how she would spend her time if she knew she had limited time to live, Nancy first emphasized what she wouldn't do:

I wouldn't spend so much time worrying.

Asked what she would do *instead* of worrying, the following ideas came to mind:

Okay, so if I knew I had a limited time to live, what would I do instead of worrying? I'd take more walks. I'd play with my dog. I'd look at more sunsets. If I wasn't worrying, I'd have more time, so I'd tie some fly fishing lures just because its fun to do. I'd spend more time with my husband hiking and bicycling in the woods just because it makes us happy to spend time together that way. I'd paint watercolors. And I guess I would put my belongings and legal papers in order so that when I died my husband wouldn't have too much difficulty sorting things out. It would be a relief for me, too, to have these things in order.

- 102 -

Nancy continued talking for a few more minutes about how she might live her life differently if she knew she had limited time left. Then she paused, and looking at me solemnly said:

> Yvonne, we *all* have limited time to live. It's just that we usually don't know exactly how long. You knew I was going to realize that when you asked me this question, didn't you?

A Symbol for the Time of Your Life
This exercise will help you discover your own unique symbol to remind you to live fully and give priority to the things that really matter to you. Read the instructions completely before doing this exercise so you won't have to interrupt yourself while in the middle of it.

 One Small Step
Find a comfortable place to sit where you will not be disturbed for the next fifteen minutes. Concentrate on your breathing until you achieve a comfortable state and feel centered in your body. Now close your eyes and gently ask your unconscious to give you a symbol that will remind you to spend your time in satisfying and heartfelt ways.

Sit quietly and notice what comes to mind after you ask yourself for a symbol. It may be an image, words, or a feeling. Once you know what it is, write or draw your symbol so that you will remember it in the future. Afterward, place it where you will see it often.

If the symbol lends itself to some specific object, feel free to substitute the object or use it in addition to your written record. Having your symbol readily visible will help you regularly reconnect to the idea that your life is by necessity time limited and therefore precious and valuable.

As time goes by, notice the effect that seeing this symbol has on your daily decisions about how to spend your time.

At the end of her therapy session, Nancy told me she had learned something important about the nature of how she now wanted to live her life, but she feared she would eventually lose this awareness. She said:

> It's strange, but if I can just remember that I am going to die someday, I know that I'll be able to worry less, enjoy myself more, feel the relief from having organized my stuff. All that would feel so good. But I don't know how to keep from forgetting that I'm going to die someday. How can I keep from forgetting this? I really need to remember it.

I asked her what she might use as a tangible symbol of the inevitability of death, something she could keep near her where she would see it every day.

Nancy paused and took a deep breath before answering:

> Well, one thing would be I could paint a little sign that said, "You're going to die!" and hang it on my bathroom mirror, but that feels too weird, and it would probably scare other people. A little skeleton would work, or even a little plastic skull like I've seen at novelty stores. Actually I like the skull idea. I'm going to get a little plastic skull and put it right next to my night table, because when I'm going to sleep at night is one of the times I do most of my worrying. And then when I wake up in the morning, the skull will be there to remind me to plan my day in a way that includes at least some of the things I would do if I remembered that I only have limited time to live. I hope the skull won't freak my husband out!

I suggested that Nancy explain to him what the skull symbolized for her.

A year later, I ran into Nancy in a local grocery store. She told me she is doing well. In fact she said, "I've been having the time of my life." The skull is still in place on her night table. When she travels away from home, Nancy takes the skull with her so that she can still have it next to her bed. Over the past year, she has painted some wonderful watercolors, had some great times with her husband, and she says that when the snow and cold sets in this winter she plans to get her papers and belongings organized.

MAKING TIME WHEN YOU DON'T HAVE TIME

My women friends and I always laugh at the common expression, "in my spare time." Like me, most of my friends juggle multiple roles and are rarely idle. And yet, my busiest friends are a living testimony to the axiom, "If you want something done, ask a busy person."

Several times a year I take a day off to attend a quilting seminar. These are strictly hands-on experiences. You bring your sewing machine, sit at large tables with other women, and sew various shapes and patterns under an instructor's guidance. The idea is for each student to begin making a new quilt in the class and finish it in the subsequent weeks and months. For people who love to make quilts, beginning a new one is a joyous and replenishing experience.

Guilty feelings are common among the students attending these quilting classes. Typical comments are, "I really don't have time to be doing this because I should be home cleaning my house," or "I should be at my office because I've got a ton of paper-work." Fortunately someone else in the seminar, usually an older woman with a wealth of life experience, inevitably responds to these expressions of guilt with compassion and wisdom: "That's probably exactly *why* you need to be doing this, honey. You need a break from all those things. Stop feeling guilty!"

Getting Control of Your Time

If you don't already own a daily calendar with lots of room to write, get yourself one! Allocating time for things you love is important when creating a joyous life that out-shines painful or traumatic past experiences. Scheduling the things that really matter to you may be the only way you will do them.

Even with a daily calendar to help you organize your schedule, allocating time for people and activities that matter to you may be difficult. Sometimes the only way to make more time is to simplify things or alter the way you approach regular tasks.

When caring for her orchid plants became a time-consuming duty instead of a source of joy, Ellen gave them away. Her friends were delighted to receive the orchids as gifts, and Ellen is equally pleased to be free of the chore of caring for them.

Once a perfectionist housekeeper, Sarah elected to have a less-than-pristine house so she could spend more time enjoying her young children. Reflecting on this, she observes, "I can always clean my house. The dirt won't go away, but my children aren't always going to be young and at home with me. I want to enjoy this time together while we can."

Marlena's favorite way to create more time in her life is something she calls multi-tasking. In between loads of laundry she returns phone calls, pays the bills, prepares dinner, and crochets afghan blocks. While not everyone would find this approach appealing, Marlena swears it makes her mundane chores more interesting and allows her to accomplish much more in less time. As a result, she has more time available to do the things she most enjoys: gardening, taking long walks, and playing card games on her home computer.

Possibilities
- What things in your life do you wish you had more time for?
- Are there tasks you might consolidate or eliminate to free yourself for other things you value or especially enjoy?

Uncluttering Your Life
Giving away items you no longer use to friends and charities clears out clutter that can slow down even the most basic and necessary daily routines. How much easier and faster would it be to get dressed in the morning if your closet no longer contained those items you rarely or never wear? What about those shoes at the back of your closet? You know the one's I'm talking about. Why not have them repaired or else discard them?

Are your kitchen shelves and drawers so crowded with duplicate versions of utensils, pots, pans, and dishes that finding what you need to prepare a meal has become a frus-trating and time-consuming process?

Sometimes recycling is as simple as packing up a cardboard box with the kitchen items you no longer need and mailing it to a young person you know who just moved into their first apartment. They will be grateful and so will you every time you put things away in the your newly spacious cupboards.

What about the decorative items in your house? Has your taste changed since you acquired certain objects? Perhaps the picture you once loved no longer brings you joy. Maybe you've been hanging onto an ugly candelabra for years even though you hate it because someone told you it was valuable. Perhaps you know someone who would love these things. Why not give these objects away and enjoy the pleasure you see on the faces of the family or friends who receive them.

Or perhaps it's time for a garage sale. One person's trash is usually someone else's treasure. You will make some money while gaining space and added simplicity in your life as your unwanted belongings find new homes.

Of course some of the things that clutter and complicate our daily life are too valuable or meaningful to be given to strangers attending a garage sale.

If you designated various belongings to people in your will, you might give some of those items away ahead of time. A gift that comes from you now will hold rich memories for the recipient.

Possibilities
- Are there special things that you no longer need that you would enjoy passing on to loved ones?

Every time I prepare a holiday meal, I am warmed by the memories connected to an old silver serving spoon I received from my grandmother one autumn afternoon many years ago. I was thrilled and so was she because, as she told me at the time, she was relieved to no longer have the responsibility of keeping it polished! My niece is nine years old, and already I am beginning to collect a small box of things that I will give her while I am still alive to see her joy.

When making choices to simplify your life beware of discarding items that hold such personal sentimental value for you as to be irreplaceable. Examples might include your baby's first lock of hair, your grandfather's shaving mug, the special card your mother gave you when you graduated, the pearl pin from your best friend. With the exception of those things that truly touch your heart, a good rule is to never hang onto a possession that is neither useful nor pleasing to your eye, hand, or ears.

FOLLOWING YOUR INTERNAL CLOCK

In his groundbreaking book, *Twenty-Minute Break*, Ernest Rossi describes Ultradian rhythms, the 90- to 120-minute cycles that most of our bodies follow. From our physical energy, appetite, and sexual feelings to our creativity, mental alertness, and emotional states, we are moving constantly through a wave-like cycle of activities followed by short periods when our mind and bodies seek rest and renewal.

Signals that we have reached the time to take a break and allow our body and mind to recharge include difficulty concentrating, memory loss, hunger, sleepiness, errors, and moodiness. If, as Rossi points out, instead of taking a break at these moments, we attempt to ignore and push through the period when our mind and body are crying out for rest, the resulting stress can lead to a host of psychosomatic illnesses, as well as increased stress and fatigue.

Drinking endless cups of coffee, smoking cigarettes, and eating sugar-laden foods are typical attempts to override our natural need for a few minutes of rest and renewal. Next time you have a craving for one of these, take a short rest break instead. Afterward, notice whether you still have a craving for caffeine, sugar, or nicotine.

Your Natural Rhythms
The following exercise will help you learn your natural Ultradian cycles.

 One Small Step
Carry a small notebook around with you for three days. Once an hour, during your waking hours, record your level of alertness and energy on a scale of 1 to 10.

Imagine that 10 means you are at your most alert, most optimum level for working. At 9 you are still alert, but not able to concentrate as effectively as at level 10. At the midpoint, 5 indicates you are neither particularly alert nor especially sleepy, a sort of neutral level. The lowest level, 1, signifies you are feeling so sleepy that it is difficult to stay awake.

Compare your hourly scores for three days to get a good idea of your natural high- and low-energy rhythms. This will help you organize daily activities to best take advantage of the times when your concentration and energy is especially high and to rest and replenish yourself during your low-energy periods.

While a twenty-minute break is ideal, shorter relaxation breaks are also beneficial. Your break at work can be as simple as sitting quietly at your desk with your eyes closed for a moment, taking a walk to the water cooler, eating a piece of fruit, or closing your door for a ten-minute nap.

As you continue to pay attention to your natural Ultradian rhythms, you will eventually be able to accurately estimate the time of day by how you feel physically and mentally instead of by looking at your watch. Your body has a wisdom of its own.

Learning to honor one's inner clock will not only lead to enhanced productivity, creativity, and concentration, it will also help prevent illness and fatigue. I have found that when I honor my Ultradian rhythms, I accomplish more yet feel less tired at the end of the day.

Since our personal rhythms do not necessarily coincide with those of our children, partners, or friends, certain compromises are required. I do my best mental work first thing in the morning. My husband is a night owl and works well in the late evening. We have learned to adjust to one another's rhythms. He refrains from discussing complicated ideas or problems late at night, and I wait until afternoon to deliberate important decisions with him.

Timelessness: Taking Time to Do "Nothing"

A friend of mine who meditates describes an experience of timelessness—a little glimpse of eternity, or what it might be like to have time stand still. An advanced practitioner of Buddhist meditation, unless he sets an alarm or looks at a clock afterward, he has no idea whether he has been meditating for five minutes or sixty minutes. Such is the nature of those ecstatic experiences that are so compelling and rewarding that time becomes irrelevant.

Although I have regularly practiced various kinds of meditation and centering techniques for the past twenty years, I have rarely had the experience my friend described.

Usually I am all too aware of time passing as I try to clear my mind of distractions. But I know what he is talking about because I have experienced that sense of timelessness or time distortion on other occasions when I was doing something that I love. For me it is usually gardening.

My husband and I live in a rural area overlooking a valley in the foothills of the Colorado Rocky Mountains. For seven months out of the year, I cannot resist beginning every morning with a walk through the garden listening to bird songs, discovering which flowers have opened, and finding out which new seeds have finally sprouted tiny green leaves.

Sometimes an hour, even two hours pass before I come back into the house, but it always feels afterward as if I have only spent a few minutes outside. Over the years, this seemingly everyday activity of walking in the garden doing nothing has become an ecstatic experience for me, a little glimpse of the boundlessness of eternity.

We all need to listen to our internal clock so that we know when to work and when to replenish ourself by doing nothing.

One Small Step

Take a moment now to consider the next twenty-four hours. Schedule a half-hour break in the next day or evening when you are not expected to do anything except relax and replenish yourself.

During this time off you are to do nothing except what pleases you, whether it's soaking in a bubble bath, reading a magazine, or simply resting. Afterward notice what difference taking this break made in the remainder of your day.

If you feel you are too busy to do this, well okay, schedule a fifteen-minute break. But frankly if you are too busy to give yourself a half-hour break, what you probably really need is a two-hour one!

Taking time off to do nothing for at least a short while every day is not a luxury, it is a necessity. A busy young attorney, Paul unfortunately had to learn this truth the hard way. Working in a high pressure job in a large legal firm, Paul had been putting in sixty- and seventy-hour weeks for over a year. Other than eating and sleeping, all his time was spent at his office working, trying to satisfy several very demanding clients. Paul knew that if he kept up this pace for another year, he would be made a partner in the firm.

And then it happened. Paul found himself sitting at his desk feeling terribly ill, unable to string one coherent thought together despite the pressure of yet another deadline. No matter how he tried, he could not concentrate on his work.

Paul called his doctor in terror. He was admitted to a mental hospital that same night. He just couldn't think, and this caused him to believe that he was losing his mind.

Paul was not losing his mind. Rather, his mind was shutting down so that sanity and the normal functions of healthy living could reemerge! Fortunately, Paul listened to the message inherent in this experience and immediately began to slow down, including making time for a life outside of work.

Eventually Paul became a partner in the law firm, but by then his work was no longer the only important thing in his life. He learned to savor friendships, hobbies, travel, and relaxation, and to listen to his body's natural rhythms and demands—which will probably lengthen his life. Paul has learned to organize his life with more respect to his internal clock.

A Child's Perspective of Time

There are some around us who are not ruled by clocks, appointments, and daily commitments. Look for people in your life who can remind you to notice the beauty of the moment you are sharing, replenishing you with a joyous break in your day.

Because their awareness is focused on the present, young children and babies offer their own particular gift to those of us who sometimes lose the knack of staying aware of the current moment. Children are very good at noticing what is around them and are more than willing to touch, taste, and smell whatever is within their reach with fearless abandon. Parents sometimes describe the experience of seeing ordinary objects as if for the first time while they vicariously enjoy their child's discovery and appreciation.

One Small Step
Think of an occasion when your attention was pleasantly absorbed by a baby or young child, and time seemed to stand still or pass effortlessly.

Possibilities
- How was this experience different from your everyday life?
- How might you benefit from incorporating some aspect of this different sense of time into your life?
- How might you do this? For example, do you want to spontaneously stop and rest or fully enjoy a sunset, a bird's song, a flower, or other common phenomena that typically occupy a child's attention? Or would you like to spend more time with children so you can observe and reclaim the timeless sense of wonder with which they experience the world?

Spending Time with Pets

I cannot end this chapter without mentioning animals and the transformative quality they can bring to the way we experience time. Numerous studies have shown that people who own and spend time with a pet have fewer heart attacks, lower blood pressure, and a more positive psychological attitude.

Just observing a pet enjoying himself is relaxing for most people. Perhaps this is because, like babies and small children, animals live in the present. They are not prisoners of a clock or hostages to work deadlines, and their presence is a reminder that we do not always need to be either.

You may own a pet, or maybe the wild birds or playful squirrels outside your office window are the only animal life in your world. Regardless of where they are, the animals that are part of your daily life can serve as potent reminders of the importance of being aware of your own natural senses as you go through life, savoring the moments as they pass. Take a moment now to think about the animals that are currently part of your life. Note how their presence can help you experience the beauty and gifts of the present.

 One Small Step

Think of an occasion when you enjoyed yourself with a pet or other animal and your attention was focusing primarily on them.

Possibilities
- How was this experience different from your everyday life?

- How might you benefit from incorporating some aspect of this different sense of time into your life?
- How might you do this? For example, would you enjoy spending time with wildlife in nature? Do you like to feed birds outdoors? Are you interested in learning to ride a horse? Do you want to devote more time to walking or playing with a special pet? Would you like to acquire and care for a pet?

This chapter has offered several ideas for enhancing your relationship with the time that belongs to you. Time will inevitably pass. It is your right and privilege to spend time and experience its passage in the ways that are most meaningful and rewarding for you. Particularly if you suffered painful or traumatic experiences in the past, it is important to remember that as long as you are alive there is still time available to nurture yourself and create rewarding new experiences that can make the present more compelling than your past.

The next chapter will provide a variety of ways for you to enhance the current relationships in your life.

PART THREE

RESPONDING TO LIFE'S CHALLENGES

CHAPTER SEVEN

PARTNERS, PARENTS, KIDS, AND EXTENDED FAMILY

Oh, life is a glorious cycle of song,
A medley of extemporanea;
And love is a thing that can never go wrong;
And I am Marie of Roumania.

—Dorothy Parker

When your own life is in order, you feel better about yourself
which makes you more clearheaded about your marriage.

—Michelle Weiner-Davis

Enjoying a good relationship is an important part of creating a satisfying life. And while anyone who has suffered a painful divorce can confirm that being in a relationship is not always wonderful, it often is. Happy times from past relationships nurture many of the hopes and dreams we bring to new relationships. This chapter will promote your ability to have a great relationship.

The first section of this chapter explores ways to enhance and strengthen relationships with a partner. The next section focuses on parents, siblings, and extended families, followed by a section discussing relationships with our children. The final section offers guidelines for protecting yourself from exploitive and abusive people.

THE COUPLE RELATIONSHIP

For many people, a long-term couple relationship offers the greatest potential for joy, pain, and growth. If you suffered emotional pain or abuse in the past, and have not yet experienced the counterbalancing effects of a caring and loving relationship, you might be tempted to avoid the hazards and emotional intimacy of a future relationships for fear of being hurt again. Don't. The rewards of loving are more than worth the risks.

Complementarity: The Attraction of Opposites

Assuming you are in a couple relationship as you read this, are you and your partner exactly alike? I doubt it. A primary relationship with no differences between the partners could quickly become dull and boring. The disparate personality traits that initially attracted you to your partner are part of what keeps a long-term relationship interesting.

There is an ecology underlying the choice of a partner or spouse. We tend to choose people whose traits and abilities fit with but also balance ours. Positive complementarity is a term family therapists use to describe relationships in which the personalities and abilities of both partners fit together in a way that benefits each person and enhances the relationship. Such complementarity is at the core of many great relationships.

Every relationship experiences positive complementarity at times, and the degree of complementarity in your relationship can be augmented. The following exercise will show you how to identify and increase the frequency of positive complementarity in your relationship.

One Small Step

Think of a time when things were going well between you and your partner; you were both happy in each other's company, fitting well together as a couple. This was an instance when you were experiencing complementarity in your relationship.

Possibilities

- What contributed to this instance of positive complementarity?
- Where were the two of you?
- What were you both doing?
- When did it occur?

Now consider replicating some or all of the same conditions. What would be the first small step? Take that step. Remember that it is not necessary to repeat precisely what you did on your special occasion. Your goal is to capture the essence of the experience.

Judy and Michael have been married for thirty years, and they still delight in each other's company. Raised on a farm in the rural south, Judy grew up in a family where simple country pleasures were valued. Michael grew up amid the hustle and bustle of New York City in a cultured, intellectual family who "talked about wonderful ideas ad infinitum but usually never got around to doing much." Judy's earthiness, practicality, humor, and country common sense was refreshing for Michael. Correspondingly, Judy was attracted to Michael's sophistication, love of the arts, and romantic "city gentleman" manners. Michael is a gourmet cook. Judy doesn't cook at all, but she grows gorgeous tomatoes, lettuces, and other vegetables that Michael enjoys using in his cooking, and she loves what he cooks. Michael doesn't garden, but he really likes it that Judy does.

Evidence of complementarity is not always as blatantly obvious as it is with Judy and Michael. Yet it is still at work in many good relationships. The best evidence of positive complementarity in a couple relationship are occasions where the partners take mutual pleasure in each other's company. The more often a couple shares common pastimes, the more likely they will feel they have a good relationship.

Marilyn and Ted recounted an idyllic vacation they spent together in Mexico a few years ago when they delighted in each other's company. They walked along the beach, stayed in a hotel, visited interesting restaurants, gave each other back rubs, had great sex, listened to the sound of the ocean in bed at night, and read books that they loved. Right now, they have neither the money nor the time to vacation in Mexico. But they could replicate one or more aspects of the experience thereby rekindling the feeling of complementarity they enjoyed there.

They could walk outdoors together. Although the beaches of Mexico are far from their Cincinnati home, they can still go for a walk near a lake or river or some other beautiful outdoor setting. They might play a tape of ocean music in their bedroom and listen again to the soothing sounds they heard in their hotel room. Or they could go to a new restaurant in their hometown without their children. This would recapture some of the novelty of visiting new restaurants in a distant country.

Other possibilities include visiting a bookstore or library to rekindle their shared love of reading or going to bed early so they aren't too tired to give each other a back rub or enjoy lovemaking.

The next section will help you cope more easily with the difficult times that happen even in the best relationships.

The Relationship Resource Inventory, or Remembering the Good Times,
Especially When You're Having a Bad Time
Recently, my husband and I were sitting in our backyard garden watching the sunset after enjoying a good meal. I was feeling especially appreciative of something he had done earlier that day, and my feelings of love and gratitude for him and our relationship were overflowing. I told him so. He really liked hearing this. Then he smiled meaningfully and said, "I hope you will remember this the next time you're mad at me." I knew what he was talking about. It's the unfortunate truth that the times we most need to remember the strengths and values of a relationship are when it's hardest to do so.

People tend to edit their storehouse of memories to support a current mood (Synder and White, 1982). When things are going well in a relationship, you will likely remember other happy and rewarding times with your partner. But when you're in a bad mood and irritated with your partner, you will often emphasize past troublesome times, ignoring shared good experiences. This can lead to further frustrations and outright conflict, and is typically how arguments between partners escalate.

The Relationship Resource Inventory will foster warm feelings about your relationship. Afterward it can be used as a psychological safety net to prevent you from disregarding the good things about your relationship when it is most difficult to remember them.

You can reread the Relationship Resource Inventory whenever you are feeling discouraged or frustrated with your partner and want to approach a problem with a positive attitude. Therefore, you should respond to the questions in terms of what your partner does as opposed to what he or she does not do.

One Small Step
List the behaviors or personality qualities about your partner that you most appreciate. Now record shared activities that you enjoy. Go into as much detail as possible.

- 120 -

While you may not feel like rereading your Relationship Resource Inventory when you and your partner are having trouble, it's worth making yourself do it anyway. As Michele Wiener-Davis points out in *Divorce Busting*, when you're making an effort to improve your relationship, "You don't have to like it, you just have to do it."

You are less likely to blow your disagreement out of proportion if you keep a problem in perspective. It's easier to solve a small problem than a large one.

Now that you have completed your Relationship Resource Inventory, how do you imagine your partner would react if you showed it to him? What do you guess your partner would write if he were to create a similar list? Whether you decide to share your Inventory with your partner or not, the emphasis you placed on acknowledging the admirable aspects of your relationship will positively color your attitude and optimally influence any future disagreements.

Who Are You Apart from All Relationships?
It may initially seem paradoxical to include a discussion about the need to develop a sense of yourself apart from your relationship in a section about couple relationships. However, a lack of a sense of self independent from a couple relationship can wreak major havoc. People with no sense of self apart from their relationship are in the terrible position of expecting their partner to meet all of their emotional needs. This places an unrealistic burden on the relationship and can lead to endless frustration and mutual resentment.

As David Schnarch points out in his excellent book, *Passionate Marriage*, a sense of self and the ability to soothe and comfort yourself independent of your significant other is crucial in order to create a fulfilling long-term relationship. This "differentiated" (Kerr and Bowen, 1988) sense of self allows partners to build a relationship based on love and strength, rather than on feelings of inadequacy and dependency.

In my early thirties I was going through a lot of pain at the breakup of a marriage. I feared that I would never love or be loved by anyone again. Worse yet, when my husband left I felt a terrifying emptiness that sometimes seemed to eclipse all sense of myself. The pain and terror of those first few days was a revelation. I remember thinking, "I never knew it was possible to feel this much pain."

What I experienced back then is an example of what can happen to a primarily undifferentiated person when their partner leaves. With the awareness that the marriage was over, I felt as if the person I was when married had now ceased to exist and so had much of the familiar sense of how I defined myself. It was ghastly.

The first few weeks after my marriage ended seemed like an endless dark night of the soul. While everyday activities of work, self-care, and conversations with other people offered a measure of relief, being alone plunged me back into an agony of grief and self-doubt.

I was puzzled and somewhat crushed by the fact that my soon-to-be-ex-husband did not seem to be experiencing anything near the soul-shaking level of pain and anxiety that I was. He was already in a new relationship and seemed to be comfortably reorganizing his life while functioning as usual at his work and in his personal life. Though I did not think of it at the time, his already being in a new relationship may well have been responsible for some of his apparent resilience. Or perhaps he was simply far more differentiated than I was.

There are many different ways that undifferentiated people resolve their agony when a significant loved one leaves or dies. Some people rebound quickly into a new serious relationship. They may feel much better, confirming the appropriateness of their choice.

Other people jump from one relationship to the next, denying themselves the opportunity to develop a sense of profound and permanent relief and stability. They remain undifferentiated and unaware of the peace and comfort they carry within themselves.

Still others simply shut down emotionally and do not allow new relationships to become deep enough to risk the kind of loss they felt before. These people tend to keep others at arm's length. They may find a long-term partner who also prefers to avoid the intensity and vulnerability that comes from loving someone ardently. Or they may prefer a series of short-term, casual relationships, or even remain loners.

Yet some people endure the anxiety of confronting their lack of differentiation long enough to develop a more stable and comforting sense of self that will stand them in good stead in future relationships.

The turning point in my own struggle with differentiation came quite unexpectedly after several long months during a visit from a good friend. After listening quietly to my tale of woe, he offered the following advice: "Figure out who you are apart from all relationships and you'll feel better." While I had no idea how to do this, the notion stayed with me.

After my friend left I began asking myself at odd moments who I was apart from all relationships. Once I got over the initial anxiety of not immediately knowing the answer, the practice of asking the question began to evoke a sort of meditative state characterized by a growing sense of internal peace and comfort.

I began to realize that just being able to ask myself this question meant I had some sense of self apart from all relationships, and yet paradoxically it also meant there was something bigger than any one relationship of which we were all part.

Then I remembered experiencing a similar response in the past when considering Zen koans, though I had not fully appreciated it at the time. Even now, nearly twenty years later, during times of inner turmoil or at times of quiet reflection, I continue to pursue the original question, "Who are you apart from all relationships?"

Gradually a satisfying answer has emerged. It is a wordless answer, so I cannot describe it in linear terms, but it is a sense of knowing that I associate with God, and it is extremely comforting. It is characterized by a physical sense of centeredness in my body, and deep, even breathing. I still struggle to keep this answer in mind when I most need to remember it: times of conflict in my marriage or times of self-doubt.

At this point, I have been married nearly fifteen years to my husband, Charlie Johnson. I feel a deep sense of appreciation and gratitude for the gift of this continuing relationship. However, life has taught me that there are no guarantees. Fate or death may someday rob me of my husband. Because I have become more differentiated, rather than spending my time fearing such things, this awareness allows me to more fully appreciate the relationship we share.

I invite you now to pause and take a moment to experience your answer to the question for yourself.

One Small Step
Set aside a half hour in a quiet place. Find a comfortable position and allow your breathing to develop an even, soothing rhythm. Then gently ask yourself, Who are you apart from all relationships?

Don't worry about finding the "right" answer, or even immediately finding a satisfying answer. Simply asking the question is valuable because it allows you to start experiencing the internal state in yourself which will eventually become your answer. Repeat this question at various intervals over the next days, weeks, and months as often as you find meaningful.

Enhancing Differentiation from Your Partner
Another way to enhance your level of differentiation is to approach it on a cognitive, intellectual level. Because some people prefer a more linear approach, I have developed an exercise that can be used on its own or as an adjunct to the Who Are You Apart from All Relationships question.

 One Small Step
Allow yourself to focus on each of the following questions separately, progressing only to the level of questions you feel able to answer at this point. You may complete this exercise in one sitting if you wish, or pursue the questions gradually over the course of days, weeks, or months, writing your answers as you determine them.

Beginning Level
1. In what ways are you similar to your partner?
2. In what ways are you different from your partner?
3. Among those personality traits or characteristics you have in common with your partner, which do you most value or like? List them.
4. Among those personality traits or characteristics you have in common with your partner, are there any that you dislike or that make you uncomfortable? If so, list them.

Intermediate Level

5. Who are you as a person apart from this relationship? How do you or could you most positively express these aspects of yourself in your daily life?

6. How can you help yourself remain relatively calm and centered during times when your partner or other significant loved one is stressed or upset?

7. What are some healthy and meaningful ways for you to soothe or take care of yourself when you are upset and your partner is unable to help?

Advanced/Mature Level

8. What would you most want to remember about your partner if he or she were no longer present, or no longer living?

9. What do you hope your partner would remember most about you if you were no longer living?

10. What do you hope the survivor will be able to remember about your relationship when death ends your time together?

Don't be concerned if initially you have difficulty answering some of the questions. Except for those rare and lucky individuals who emerge from a nurturing childhood with a profound sense of self and the resulting ability to soothe themselves regardless of what is going on in their life, differentiation is something that must be earned by rising to the challenges and difficulties that a relationship presents.

And don't worry if you can't immediately access all your newly discovered personal resources when relationship snarls occur. Differentiation is a gradual developmental process that most of us continue to pursue (or avoid!) unconsciously or consciously all our lives. The more differentiated we become, the more we are able to stay clearheaded, remaining flexible and resourceful in our relationships and in tolerating, containing, and eventually moving beyond the inevitable anxiety that occurs during stressful life events.

YOUR FAMILY OF ORIGIN

In order to become more differentiated in your relationship with your partner, it is sometimes necessary to first strengthen your ability to maintain a sense of self that is distinct and independent from your parents and the rest of the family in which you grew up. The next exercise will help you strengthen this ability.

Enhancing Differentiation from Your Family of Origin

 One Small Step

Allow yourself to focus on each of the following questions separately, progressing only to the level of questions that you feel able to answer at this point. You may complete this exercise in one sitting if you wish, or pursue the questions gradually over the course of days, weeks, or months, writing your answers as you determine them.

Beginning Level

1. In what ways are you similar to each of your parents or childhood caregivers?
2. In what ways are you different from each of them?
3. Among those personality traits or characteristics you have in common with each parent or childhood caregiver, which do you most value or like? What is the most satisfying and healthy way for you to express this in everyday life?
4. Among those personality traits or characteristics you have in common with each parent or childhood caregiver, which ones do you value least? What is the most healthy and productive way for you to manage or express or transform these characteristics?

Intermediate Level

5. Who are you as a person apart from your relationship with your parents or other childhood caregivers? How do you or could you most positively express these aspects of yourself in your daily life?
6. How can you help yourself remain relatively calm and centered during times when one of both of your parents (or childhood caregivers) are stressed or upset?

7. What are some healthy and meaningful ways for you to soothe or take care of yourself when you are upset and your parents (or other childhood caregivers) are unable to help?

Advanced/Mature Level
8. What do you want to remember about your parents when they are no longer living?
9. What do you hope your parents would remember most about you if you were no longer living?

This exercise can also be used with siblings, extended family, and friends.

As with the Enhancing Differentiation from Your Partner questions, don't worry if you don't find all of the questions easy to answer. However, if any of the questions evoke severe anxiety, consider whether you might benefit from pursuing the issue with a psychotherapist's support. And as with your partner, it may take time before you can access your personal resources at times of stress, loss, or crisis with your family.

Moving Beyond Old Issues with a Parent
As an adult, Daniel was still hampered by anger toward his parents. He told me,

> I wasted a lot of time blaming my parents for the fact that I wasn't living the kind of life I wanted. Not that some blame wasn't warranted. They made a lot of mistakes in the way they raised me, some of them real bad ones. My father used to beat me, and my mother criticized me all the time and never noticed anything I did right. But spending my time blaming them after I became an adult took up energy that I needed to make a good life for myself.

Unfortunately, reclaiming the energy we spend continuing to blame our parents is easier said than done, especially when the resentment stems from childhood abuse. If unresolved feelings about your parents are interfering with your ability to focus on creating a good life for yourself, the following exercise will help.

One Small Step

Allow at least a half hour to complete this exercise. Find a comfortable position and allow an image of your parent to form in your mind. You will need three pieces of paper and something to write with.

1. On the first piece of paper, list everything you resent about your parent.
2. On a separate piece of paper, list everything you appreciate about your parent. Remember to include anything you learned from your parent.
3. Considering your first two lists, record on a third piece of paper those aspects of your relationship that you appreciate and would like to continue to influence your current life or your current relationship with your parent.
4. Now burn pages 1 and 2, and reread page 3.

Strengthening Your Relationship with Your Parents

This exercise can be done immediately after completing the previous one or at a later time when you wish to focus on the positive aspects of your relationship with your parents.

One Small Step

Allow at least a half hour to complete this exercise. Find a comfortable position and allow an image of your parents to form in your mind. You will need paper and something to write with.

1. Record those aspects of the time you currently spend with your parents that you want to remember when you are their age.
   (If your parents are no longer alive and you are experiencing unresolved feelings of hurt or resentment toward them, substitute the Healing Letters exercise in the next chapter.)
2. Now list what you hope they would remember most about this same time.
3. Write down the aspects of the relationship you would like to continue.
4. If you have had recent conflicts with your parents, record what was different about the times when there was less conflict or things were more comfortable between you. How might you contribute to making such times occur more frequently?

The above two exercises can be used to address unresolved feelings toward siblings, extended family, and other important people from your past.

When Parents Continue to Be Hurtful
If you find yourself feeling overwhelmed and anxious when you are with your parents, try using the following technique.

 One Small Step
Imagine that twenty or thirty years have passed and your parents are no longer alive. How would you wish to have spent the times when you were with them during those intervening years?

Asking yourself this question will assess your current time spent with your parents from the viewpoint of an adult, rather than slipping into the thinking that characterized the powerless child you once were.

Judy had long ago given up focusing on the pain she had endured while growing up with alcoholic and abusive parents. She had devoted her energy first to a successful career as a teacher, later to her marriage, and then to providing a nurturing environment for her five-year-old son.

She loved her teaching job, was happy in her marriage, and felt delight watching her young son grow and discover the world around him. Judy considered herself lucky. The painful childhood she had endured made her present contentment and joy all the more precious.

Several times a year, during the Thanksgiving, Christmas, and Easter holidays, Judy and her small family journeyed across the country to visit her aging parents. She dreaded these visits, but continued them out of a sense of duty. "After all," she told herself, "they are my parents. I owe them this." Her husband did not enjoy these visits, but he respected Judy's need to spend time with her family. His own parents had died earlier in his adult life.

On each visit, Judy's father would belittle Judy and her husband's professional and educational accomplishments. Her mother constantly criticized Judy's choice of clothing and the way she was raising her son. When Judy pointed out to her parents that their belittling and criticizing behavior was hurtful, they ridiculed her as being overly sensitive and unable to accept the "truth" about herself.

Throughout the visits, her mother would reminisce about Judy's childhood, talking about all the wonderful times she remembered. Her husband's beatings and her own alcoholic lapses and verbal abuse were deleted from these idealized descriptions. When Judy would gently remind her mother that there had been some difficult times also, her mother would angrily tell Judy what a pitiful, ungrateful excuse for a daughter she was.

As each holiday approached, Judy would become increasingly depressed. She became irritable with her husband and son, and impatient with her students. She began to wake in the middle of the night asking herself, "Why am I doing this?" The answer was, "Because I feel I have no choice but to go on visiting my parents. And I don't want to go."

Finally, alarmed by suicidal feelings, Judy visited a psychotherapist. She did not want to kill herself, but she had reached the point at which she could not face another painful visit with her parents. The therapist suggested counseling that would include Judy and her parents. When Judy proposed this to her parents, they angrily refused.

The therapist observed to Judy, "You can't control what they do, but you can control what you do. When you are an old woman and they are no longer alive, how do you imagine you will want to have spent these next twenty years?"

In response to that question, Judy decided that as an old woman she would want to remember some happy holidays alone in her own home with her husband and son and their friends. As a result she decided to limit visits to her parents to twice a year. She would send them loving cards and letters on the holidays, but she would no longer expose herself and her family to their emotional battering at the times of year when she most wanted to enjoy herself.

Judy also decided to limit the duration of visits to her parents to two days. This was the amount of time that she could handle without becoming seriously depressed. Since interactions with her parents seemed to go better when there were planned activities, she arranged to visit museums and attend movies while visiting them and invited them to accompany her if they chose.

A few years after making these decisions, Judy told me,

I feel I have worked things out with my parents as well as I can. When I was growing up they did some kind and good things for me as well as the abusive things. I love them because they are my parents. But I will not allow them to make me miserable and even suicidal as an adult. My responsibility these days is to my own family: my husband, my child, and myself.

As a child, any attempt to limit the pain her parents caused her had only brought Judy more abuse. While living under her parents' roof, Judy had no choice but to comply with their demands and to accept their abusive behavior. However, as an adult she had the power to decide how and when she wanted to interact with her parents.

If your parents behave hurtfully toward you at this point in your life, letting them know that you find certain behaviors painful may result in them changing. If not, you might propose family counseling, or like Judy you might choose to alter the way you spend time with them.

YOUR CHILDREN

The following exercise will help you apply the principles and ideas from the earlier sections of this chapter to your relationships with your children. If you have children or you are a caregiver for a child, take a moment now to answer the following questions.

 One Small Step

Allow at least a half hour to complete this exercise. Find a comfortable position and allow an image of your child to form in your mind.

- What do you most appreciate about your child?
- What aspects of your relationship do you most want to continue?
- If you have conflicts or problems with your child, what was different about the times when there was less conflict or things were more comfortable between you? How might you arrange to have these times occur more frequently?
- When your children are the age you are now, what do you want them to look back and remember about this time in your relationship?

Again, I recommend recording your answers to the questions. You can review them whenever you want to remember what is special about your child. And undoubtedly, if you repeat the exercise at distant intervals, your answers will be a history of the growth of your relationship.

The exercises in the next section of this chapter will help you identify and control the effects that painful past experiences may be having on your relationships with your children, your partner, or other important people in your life.

THE EFFECT OF PAST PAIN ON CURRENT RELATIONSHIPS

Have you ever felt that you are placing more importance on a casual relationship or a minor aspect of a more important relationship than it warrants? One of the legacies of trauma and abuse that can especially effect relationships is the tendency to fluctuate between idealized and overly critical views of yourself and other people, and to under-emphasize or overemphasize certain characteristics to justify these views. The result is often a phenomenon called *transference*.

In Woody Allen's movie *Annie Hall*, there is a scene in which two lovers are in bed together seemingly sharing an intimate moment. However they are not alone. Images of each of their respective family members and ex-lovers are superimposed on the scene.

In this way, the cinematographer humorously depicts the excess emotional baggage each of them brings to their relationship through transference. Transference refers to unconsciously ascribing or "transferring" feelings and assumptions you had about one significant person in your life to someone else.

The following exercise will help you identify, control, and eventually undo the effects of transference in your current relationships. In the future you will base your responses on accurate information about the person you are dealing with rather than on old feelings about someone else.

One Small Step
Set aside thirty minutes to write your answers to the following questions. Think of a person in your life toward whom you have or once had immediate and intense positive or negative feelings. Take a moment to picture this person in your mind, what they looked and sounded like.

1. Does this person remind you in any way of someone significant from your past? Does some aspect of your relationship with this person remind you of any experience in your past that elicited similar emotions?
2. If you answered "yes" to either of the above questions, make a list of how the person or situation in the present is similar to the person or situation from the past. Do these similarities provide any clues as to how you might best deal with the present situation? For example, what was helpful in the past?
3. Now list how the present person or situation differs from the past person or situation.
4. Based on these differences, how might you most fairly and effectively deal with the present person? Now you can begin to adjust your behavior toward them accordingly.

The person to whom you direct these feelings usually has some resemblance to the person who evoked the feelings. However, at least some of the beliefs and feelings that you associate with the new person are likely to be inaccurate. Transference can prevent us from perceiving and appreciating the unique qualities of our loved ones. Transference can also render us vulnerable to disappointment and exploitation.

For example, if you had a loving relationship with an immigrant grandfather, transference might cause you to automatically feel kindly toward other paternalistic males with foreign accents before considering their actual character traits. I once met a sociopathic building contractor who had swindled many people. When I hired him I didn't know this history. Something about the "goodness" I imagined I perceived in him prevented me from checking his credentials.

Later, I realized the virtue I thought I had seen in him was really my reexperiencing a feeling I had in childhood with my great-grandfather who spoke with a soft French accent and had beautiful white hair. Because of the similarity of having a foreign accent and white hair, I had unconsciously transferred these warm pleasant feelings to the contractor without assessing their accuracy.

When I learned subsequently of the corrupt and exploitive things the contractor had done to many other clients, I felt angry and betrayed. When I realized how different the contractor was from my great-grandfather, the transference was undone. I could then see the contractor clearly. I realized that he showed little integrity in his business dealings, and had only had a superficial resemblance to the relative I had loved. Thankfully, this realization allowed me to prevent the contractor from further exploiting me financially.

While I transferred positive feelings to a person who did not merit them, transference can also cause you to experience unjustified negative feelings toward people. When someone exhibits a personality trait, physical appearance, or gesture, or creates a situation that subconsciously reminds you of a painful past experience, the resulting transference can tarnish your feelings toward them even though they have done nothing to deserve it.

This phenomenon is especially tragic and damaging when parents transfer or "project" negative feelings from the past onto their innocent and vulnerable young children. Learning to identify and take responsibility for your transference tendencies will help prevent you from causing untoward pain to your own children and others you care about.

Overidealization

Overidealizing other people sets you up to be disappointed. No one is perfect, and close examination of yourself or another person usually reveals that rather quickly. People who seem "too good to be true" may in fact be exactly that.

Realizing belatedly that a friend is not as perfect as you once thought can result in feelings of betrayal. Therefore it is important to understand the difference between being disappointed by someone's failure to live up to your expectations and actually being betrayed by someone. If your feelings result solely from someone's inability to live up to your idealized assumptions about them, remind yourself that your expectations of perfection were unrealistic. Realizing this and acting accordingly can prevent you from unfairly alienating the other person and prematurely ending a potentially rewarding friendship.

One Small Step
Think of someone with whom you have repeatedly been or currently are upset. Take a moment to examine whether your feelings are the result of an unrealistic expectation about that person.

Possibilities
- How might you adjust your expectations to more accurately reflect what you know to be true of that person?
- What, if anything, do you want or hope for in this relationship?
- Would it be helpful to discuss your goals openly with the other person?

Abusive and Exploitive People

Another problem with idealizing people is that you can become vulnerable to unscrupulous individuals who want to take advantage of you. An example is a corrupt businessperson who first develops and then exploits customers' trust in order to financially defraud them.

Some people are also emotional exploiters. They may initially present themselves as trustworthy and caring. However, their goal with friendships or other relationships is solely to benefit themselves. They often reveal themselves as emotional exploiters by being extremely selfish.

For instance, when an emotional exploiter is not in control of a situation—when they do not feel superior in an interaction with you or when you do not give them their way—they are likely to become angry. They may become verbally abusive in an effort to bully you into giving them their way, or they may threaten to end the relationship in an effort to manipulate you.

They are able to prey on people who idealize them because such illusions make their victims gullible and overly trusting. If you encounter an abusive or exploitive person in your life, and chances are you will at some time or another, it is important to set limits with them and stand up for yourself. Recognize their anger for what it is: an attempt to coerce you into complying with their demands.

Possibilities
- Is there someone in your life who has betrayed your trust or is attempting to exploit, bully, or manipulate you into doing something that is not in your best interest?
- Do you fear that not acceding to their demands would jeopardize your relationship with them? If so, imagine looking back on your life from the future

and ask yourself, Do you wish you had stood up for yourself or your principles and refused to comply with their conditions?

If you are having trouble assessing your situation, writing your thoughts out or talking to a trusted friend can help you explore your feelings. Consider seeking the expertise of an attorney or a psychotherapist if you need professional advice.

The Trap of Cynicism

If you have been exploited or abused in a past relationship, you may become distrustful and cynical and close yourself off from new relationships. This is tragic; it plants seeds of bitterness and loneliness. One way to protect yourself from the trap of cynicism is to allow yourself to trust people gradually and to avoid placing yourself in vulnerable situations with people you don't yet know well.

The following two questions can help you read the safety level of situations requiring your trust.

 Possibilities
- How well do I really know this person?
- How do I objectively know that what he or she is saying is true?

This chapter has offered a variety of strategies for overcoming the effects of past trauma and other painful life experiences on your current relationships. However, the final legacy of improving your ability to have good relationships extends far beyond overcoming negative effects of your past. You are making room for continuing and heartfelt relationships with many joyous experiences.

The next chapter will help you prevent past experiences from detracting from your quality of life and your relationships, now and in years to come.

CHAPTER EIGHT

COPING WHEN THE PAST REARS ITS UGLY HEAD

The Buddha said, "A man walking along a high road sees a great river, its near bank dangerous and frightening, its far bank safe. He collects sticks and foliage, makes a raft, paddles across the river, and reaches the other shore. Now suppose that, after he reaches the other shore he takes the raft and puts it on his head and walks with it on his head wherever he goes..."

—Stephen Mitchell

Like the raft, painful past experiences can become an emotional weight that you carry around with you, a burden that interferes with your ability to move freely and enjoy your life. This chapter will help you free yourself of unwanted baggage from the past, while reaping the benefits of strengths and skills you acquired as a result of coping with painful experiences. The first section will teach you how to unload intrusive images left over from past traumas. The second section addresses unresolved issues with past relationships. And the final section helps you take advantage of what you have learned from your traumatic episodes in your life. The exercises in this chapter will free a significant amount of your energy.

FLASHBACKS

Sometimes traumatic or painful experiences from the past show up in the form of *flashbacks*, moments comprised of intrusive thoughts and images. Besides being unpleasant and upsetting these incidents can interfere with your concentration and ability to participate fully in the current moment.

Coming into contact with people or situations that directly or indirectly remind you of unpleasant past experiences can trigger flashbacks. Seemingly unrelated experiences in the present can also trigger a flashback if something about the experience evokes feelings of vulnerability or anxiety that are similar to those you experienced in the past.

Have you ever suffered from unpleasant intrusive thoughts or images? Most people do at one time or another. For example, if you were in a car accident or had a near collision one afternoon on your way home from work, you may have found that later in the evening as you began to relax or go to sleep, images of the other car or sounds of squealing tires intrude into your consciousness.

Some people suffer recurrent unwanted thoughts or images. Others experience them infrequently, only after a similarly traumatic event resurrects memories of the past.

I met Claire the day after she witnessed her partner being robbed at gunpoint outside their car. Although neither of them had been physically harmed, the situation had been extremely frightening for both of them and resulted in upsetting and unwelcome images typical of posttraumatic stress.

A few hours after the robbery, as they tried to relax in the safety of their home, Claire and her partner found themselves involuntarily reliving the experience with the robber. Images of the robber's masked face and his outstretched arm pointing a gun kept returning along with their accompanying feelings of terror as they had wondered, "Is he going to kill us? What is he going to do to us after he gets the money?"

As is often the case with posttraumatic stress, Claire relived the experience repeatedly that night and the next day. After she described what had happened to her, I taught Claire the Write, Read, and Burn exercise. It proved effective for Claire as well as for her partner whom she taught it to later that evening.

Write, Read, and Burn

Because of its simplicity and brevity, the Write, Read, and Burn exercise is typically the first intervention I suggest to people requesting relief from intrusive thoughts and traumatic images. Developed at the Brief Family Therapy Center in Milwaukee, this method provides fairly rapid relief for most people.

One Small Step
Find a comfortable place to sit where you will not be disturbed. You will need a piece of paper, a writing tool, and a lighter or matches.

1. Write a description of the intrusive image(s) or thought(s).
2. Read the description aloud to a supportive person, or if no one is available read it aloud to yourself while imagining the support of someone you know would be a compassionate listener.
3. Now take the paper with the description of the intrusive thoughts or images, tear it up, and burn it.

Reading the description of unwelcome images aloud and then burning the paper interrupts the pattern of intrusive thoughts by symbolically providing a new ending and resolution to the traumatic event being remembered.

You can repeat the Write, Read, and Burn exercise if such images bother you again. The Write, Read, and Burn exercise may provide full relief from your unwanted images. Or you may need to repeat it often so new images don't replace old, burned ones.

You may also find that this exercise works best if followed by the Drawing Relief exercise, the Rewriting Old Messages exercise, and/or the Healing Letters exercise in the next sections of this chapter.

Drawing Relief
You may especially like the Drawing Relief exercise if you like to draw or paint and might prefer it to the Write, Read, and Burn technique. Although it is an adaptation of a technique originally developed for children (Crowley and Mills, 1986), many adults find the Drawing Relief exercise a satisfying way to interrupt the intrusive flow of negative thoughts and provide a healing resolution by creating a new, more affirming ending. Like the previous exercise, this one is not difficult and typically provides fairly rapid relief.

One Small Step

You will need drawing paper and colored pencils, crayons, colored markers, or paints. Allow at least an hour of free time. You are going to draw or paint three pictures in three steps.

1. Draw a picture of the image or feelings you associate with the intrusive thoughts. Use whatever colors best evoke this for you. Don't worry about how you choose to represent this artistically. You may draw a literal image or create an abstract representation of lines, shapes, and colors. However you express it is the right way because it is your way.

2. On a separate piece of paper, draw a second picture depicting the absence of the intrusive images. This represents what you would prefer to be feeling or thinking instead of the unwanted subjects. Again, don't worry about style, but concentrate on expressing your chosen thought or feeling in any way that fits for you.

3. On a third piece of paper, draw a new picture symbolizing how you imagine you got from the state of mind depicted in the first picture to the state of mind depicted in the second picture.

4. Now tear up the first picture.

Linda was emotionally abused by one of the teachers in her college art department. When she rebuffed his sexual advances, he began attacking her work in class. Rather than providing constructive criticism, he ridiculed her work and humiliated her in front of fellow students.

Through dogged determination, Linda was able to endure her teacher's repeated verbal attacks long enough to pass his class and complete a graduate degree in art. Although the experience had shaken her confidence, she never stopped painting in her free time, and began to regain some of her confidence as colleagues recognized and appreciated her work.

But when Linda was eventually invited to display her work in a juried art show, the abuse inflicted by the sadistic teacher reared its ugly head in the form of a painful flashback. Linda found herself vividly remembering the teacher's devastating words, "Your work is frivolous, notable only for its evidence of your singular lack of talent." But the most disturbing aspect of the flashback was the image of the contemptuous expression on her teacher's face. Unbidden, this image kept returning to Linda, unraveling her hard-earned self-confidence.

Because drawing and painting were her favorite means of self-expression, I suggested that Linda try the Drawing Relief exercise to get rid of the unwanted (and inaccurate!) message she had internalized.

First Linda drew a picture of herself as a young student with the critical teacher standing over her. In this picture he was much larger than her. In her second picture, Linda drew an image of herself standing in front of an exhibition of her paintings with a serene and happy expression on her face.

In her third picture, the one illustrating how she got from her first picture to her second picture, Linda drew herself surrounded by a circle of supportive and encouraging teachers and colleagues that she knew now or had known in the past. The abusive teacher was depicted standing outside the circle unable to get near Linda. In this picture he was smaller than Linda's colleagues and other teachers and was smaller than the image of Linda.

Then Linda tore up the first picture and kept the other two, looking at them whenever she felt vulnerable about the approaching art exhibition. Participating in the exhibit was a healing experience for her and a turning point in her career.

Rewriting Negative Messages
Inaccurate and unwanted negative messages from parents, caregivers, teachers, and other authority figures sometimes inadvertently become part of our self-image. If the teacher's negative message about the value of her work had been the dominant feature of Linda's traumatic flashback rather than the expression on his face, I would have suggested she try the following exercise which is an adaptation of a technique first created by Lucia Capacchione.

One Small Step

Consider what negative or destructive message from your past interferes with your confidence or your positive feelings about your life. Now think of a new and healthy message you would like to receive instead. Write the new message first with your dominant, then with your nondominant hand several times until it begins to feel like a familiar part of your belief system.

Using the nondominant hand as well as the one you normally write with connects the message to your right brain, the hemisphere neurologists believe to be associated with unconscious processes. Assuming you took in a negative message on an unconscious as well as a conscious level, using both hands to write the same message more fully integrates the corrective information.

The impact of this new healthy message can be strengthened by writing it repeatedly. Don't worry if the positive message doesn't feel "real" or accurate the first few times you write it; it will gradually surface in your behavior and the way you think about yourself and your life.

Marly, a talented pianist, took great joy in her continuing study and mastery of exquisite classical pieces. However, whenever her husband or friends asked her to play for them, she found herself frozen with anxiety, remembering her father's angry words.

Marly had been six years old, struggling to learn the simple melody of that week's piano lesson. A severe alcoholic, her father was home that afternoon trying to sleep off a vicious hangover. When he was awakened by the sound of the piano, he became enraged and screamed at the little girl, "You can't even play a simple tune, you idiot! Shut the door. Nobody wants to hear you."

I asked Marly to imagine what message she would like to install to replace the painful one she remembered from the past.

After considering this for a few moments, she thought of the words she tells her daughter as she practices her weekly piano lessons: "You're getting better every time you play, and it makes me so happy to hear you."

Marly wrote out the new message for herself first with her dominant hand and then with her nondominant hand, repeating this process at various intervals throughout the next few days until the message began to feel natural and comfortable to her.

UNFINISHED RELATIONSHIPS

Intrusive thoughts and images may be accompanied by powerful feelings specifically associated with a significant person from your past. Your relationship with that person often feels "unfinished" or somehow incomplete.

In her poignant and humorous book about a daughter coming to terms with conflicting feelings and memories of her mother, *Divine Secrets of the Ya-Ya Sisterhood*, Rebecca Wells describes the effects of powerful emotional memories on a young woman trying to enjoy an evening walk:

> *Although she carried a flashlight, and the light of the moon was strong, if she wasn't careful, the very vividness of her memories would cause her to lose her footing.*

Wells's character had the benefit of family and friends to support her in coming to terms with her emotional baggage from the past. Unfortunately, such support is not always available to us.

Resolving issues from the past that involve another person can become more complicated if their participation is required. Even if you are ready to seek the relief that comes from actively working to get rid of your emotional baggage, the other people involved may not share your motivation. The person from your past may be unwilling or physically or mentally unavailable to work things out with you.

Carla was sexually abused by her grandfather. Though several years had passed, she still struggled with feelings of hurt and anger about the abuse. Understandably, she wanted him to acknowledge what he had done and to express remorse for the pain he had caused her. However it was clear that this would never happen. He was in the advanced stages of Alzheimer's disease and could not recognize family members, much less think responsibly and reasonably about what Carla wished to discuss with him.

In other situations, the person with whom you have past issues may no longer be present in your life or may no longer be living. When Jason was a teenager, his father died suddenly in an accident. Prior to the accident, Jason and his dad had been struggling with one another. His dad disapproved of Jason's membership in a local street gang. Jason was angry at his dad for divorcing his mom. Now five years later, Jason is aware of many pleasant as well as painful memories about his dad.

Jason used to waiver between remembering his dad as all good or all bad. Neither view was accurate. Furthermore, he had never had the opportunity to speak his peace to his dad, and to say good-bye. He longed for the sense of closure this would bring.

The person who wronged you may not be willing to try to resolve things with you. Kathy's marriage had ended when her husband, Dave, suddenly left her and their two preschool children for a relationship with another woman. He gave her no explanation. Even years afterward, he still refused to discuss what had happened. After the divorce, Kathy began to date other men, but when a relationship grew serious, unresolved feelings toward Dave would interfere. Kathy found herself taking out the anger and distrust left over from her marriage on her new partner.

Roberta had unresolved anger toward her stepfather. He had sexually abused her younger sisters and physically abused her mother. Despite the fact that the abuse had been witnessed by several family members, her stepfather still denied it. He was not psychologically available for the women to resolve their issues with him.

The Healing Letters exercise is a powerful method for resolving pain from unfinished relationships like the ones I have just described. Because it is not possible to predict the availability or degree of cooperation of people from your past, the Healing Letters do not rely on their participation to be effective.

The Healing Letters will allow you to move forward psychologically in ways that would not be possible if you had to depend on responses from the person who wronged you. When the other person *is* available and willing to work with you to resolve past issues, these letters can serve as psychological preparation for your real conversations with them.

Completing the Healing Letters exercise will help free you from negative messages or beliefs about what was done to you—inaccurate internalized messages about yourself that you unconsciously and uncritically adopted as a result of abuse or trauma.

Your Healing Letters
Please read all the instructions in this section before beginning the Healing Letters exercise.

The Healing Letters were designed to be written. As an alternative, you can speak them aloud, or compose them in your mind. Typically, however, people achieve the most powerful results from writing them.

Address your letters to the person(s) toward whom you have unresolved feelings. Don't write your letters with the intent of mailing them; instead free yourself to write whatever you want or need to say. (After completing your Healing Letters, you may mail one if you want to. However, anticipating the letter's effect while you are writing it could interfere with its therapeutic effect by inhibiting your self-expression.)

The Healing Letters exercise is divided into four parts. Letter 1 can be completed by itself in one sitting. Letters 2 and 3 are to be written at the same time; Letter 3 must be written *immediately* after Letter 2. This is to ensure that this process is therapeutic rather than traumatic. Letter 4 may be completed at a separate time.

Reserve one hour for Letter 1, two hours for Letters 2 and 3 combined, and one hour for Letter 4. The time writing particular letters will vary depending on your style of processing and the complexity of the past relationship or situation you are addressing in your letter. The letters are commonly completed over three consecutive days, but you are welcome to give yourself more time between sessions.

The Healing Letters can be repeated as needed to increase your feelings of resolution, and further clear away any burdensome feelings that remain from your past. If for any reason, writing these letters triggers feelings that you find overwhelming, do not hesitate to reach out for help in moving past your pain or anger. You deserve the aid and comfort of other people. If support is not readily available in your personal life, contact a professional counselor or psychotherapist and schedule an appointment.

One Small Step
Letter 1. Releasing Unresolved Thoughts and Feelings

> Address this letter to the person for whom you have unresolved feelings or issues. Describe how knowing this person has effected you, including the impact of their words or actions. Include a statement of what you would like from this person in response to your letter.

The purpose of this letter is for you to articulate and further acknowledge any thoughts or feelings you have about what happened in the past relationship that still hurts you.

One Small Step
Letter 2. Releasing Internalized Negative Messages

Write an imaginary response from the person you wrote to in Letter 1. Reflect any fears you have about what the person might say back to you, as well as any fears you have about their refusing to listen or to try to understand what you communicated in Letter 1. Once written, it is important that you do not dwell on Letter 2, but move *immediately* to Letter 3.

The purpose of the second letter is to get rid of any negative beliefs or messages about yourself that were internalized as a result of what this person did to you.

 One Small Step
Letter 3. Releasing Internalized Hopes

Write a different imaginary response from the person who wronged you. Unlike in Letter 2, reflect your hopes and wishes about how the other person might respond. Communicate his or her willingness to take responsibility for what they did to you, expressing their remorse in a compassionate response to the resentment you brought up in Letter 1.

The purpose of Letter 3 is to provide the healing resolution that comes with the response you would have liked or once hoped to actually receive.

 One Small Step
Letter 4. Releasing Yourself

Write a final letter to the person who hurt you. Respond to what they said in Letter 3, reflecting the changes and resolution it afforded you. Include any final business that you left unsaid in Letter 1 or have since thought of.

You may write this letter immediately after Letter 3, or wait several days, weeks, or even months.

Remember that no two people will write the same letters even if they are addressing the same wrongdoer. The best indications of your having written successful Healing Letters are your feelings of peace and comfort afterward.

Healing Letters in Action

Because of old pain and resentment stemming from her stepfather's abuse, it was hard for Roberta to trust her boyfriend, and at times she became inappropriately angry with him. Examining these feelings, she realized that she was transferring unresolved feelings about her stepfather onto her current relationship. Writing the Healing Letters allowed Roberta to free herself from this emotional burden and to move on to enjoy a good relationship with her boyfriend.

Sample Letter 1. (Roberta wrote to her stepfather describing what he had done, how she felt, and what [if anything] she wanted from him.)

> Dear Roger,
>
> You sexually abused my little sisters and cousins, and you physically abused my mother. Over the years I kept hoping you would choose to tell the truth and say that you are sorry for what you did. I am still very angry at you because you hurt them so badly. It has been very painful for me to see the results of what you did to them. Not just your molesting them, but the message it sent them: that their feelings didn't count. Each of them has had trouble believing in herself and hasn't had the confidence to succeed at doing what she wants in her life. As a result their lives have been very hard. They have had trouble holding down jobs and have had a history of choosing men who batter them just like you did Mom.
>
> You have always refused to tell the truth and refused to say you were sorry even years later when they tried to talk to you. By continuing to lie, you made it even more difficult for them to move beyond the effects of your abuse. This makes me feel very angry and very sad. And seeing the results of what you did to them has made it hard for me to trust other men in my life, even kind and good men from my church group, because I have feared that they would behave like you.

I am writing this because I want you to tell the truth about what you did. I want you to say you were sorry so that my sisters and my mother and I can forgive you.

I was going to add to the previous sentence, "so that we can all move on with our lives." But the fact is, I have decided I am going to move on with my life with or without your apology. You are *not* going to ruin my life in the future.

Sincerely,
Roberta

Sample Letter 2. (Roberta imagined and wrote out the following response from Roger to release any fears or negative messages she may have internalized and taken in unconsciously.)

Dear Roberta,

Not for the first time, I am appalled by your crazy, distorted perceptions. You are trying to blame your own screwups and your mother's and sisters' failures in life on imagined childhood abuse at my hands. I never did anything to them or to your cousins. And I never did anything to hurt your mother. They are lying, just like you. You are just trying to hurt me and to interfere with my relationship with your mother.

I am glad that I never have to see you again.

Sincerely,
Roger

Sample Letter 3. (Roberta wrote the following imaginary response from Roger as a way of releasing her old hopes and longings about what she needed him to say to her to provide her with closure and psychological resolution.)

Dear Roberta,

I felt deeply sad after reading your letter and realizing the terrible effects of what I did. I am deeply sorry for the things I did that hurt your mother and your sisters and cousins and that hurt you. I want you to know that I did not think at the time that what I was doing to your mother and to those little girls would have the awful impact it did on them and on you. I believe if I had thought about that I would not have molested them, and I never would have hit your mother.

I know I can never make up for what I did, but I am trying to help by supporting your sisters and your cousins in paying for their counseling and their efforts to heal. I have told your mother I am sorry. I hope that you and they will find it in your hearts to forgive me. I wish you well. I wish you a good life, one that makes up for the bad things that happened in our family when you were a kid.

Sincerely,
Roger

Sample Letter 4. (Roberta responded to Letter 3 to further her resolution and closure.)

Dear Roger,

Thank you for your willingness to hear what I had to say, and for your response. It makes a difference for me. My heart feels a little lighter. I wish you God's light and peace on the rest of your life journey.

Sincerely,
Roberta

BENEFITING FROM YOUR PAST

Allen, a thirty-two-year-old teacher, was physically assaulted by two strangers who had beaten him up for no apparent reason. He explained his reason for scheduling a psychotherapy appointment with me:

> I've always felt that things happen for a reason, but I can't figure out how I have anything good to show for what those two guys did to me, beating me up in that parking lot. I keep asking myself, "Why did this happen?"

I gently suggested to him that sometimes bad things happen to good people for no apparent reason, and that this is one of the mysteries and tragedies of the human condition. While some people find comfort in the idea that bad things can happen to people in a seemingly random fashion, I could tell immediately that this was not a helpful concept for Allen.

While Allen understood what I meant, this viewpoint did not provide the resolution and completion he needed to move on with his life. He said:

> Intellectually I know what you're saying is true, but it doesn't work for me emotionally. I need to find or make some useful meaning out of what happened, even if there is no objective way to prove it.

Recognizing a River You Have Crossed

Surviving a traumatic experience is like crossing a river: while fending for yourself you develop new skills that can help you in the future. I created the following exercise for people like Allen who want to reap the benefits of identifying and figuring out how to use what they have learned as a result of surviving a painful experience.

 One Small Step

Set aside at least an hour for this exercise. Think of a painful experience that you have survived and briefly describe it.

1. What did you learn from surviving this experience?
2. What strengths or talents did you draw on then or develop later to survive the experience?
3. How can these strengths or talents be used to your best advantage now?

Carla, a successful attorney in her midforties was sexually abused as a child by her grandfather. She explained her dilemma to me:

When my grandfather was abusing me I was so hurt and overwhelmed by the experience that it sort of took over who I was. Later in college, my life became a series of survivor group meetings and political activities aimed at educating people and preventing kids from being abused. The work was very meaningful and still is, but I don't want it to continue to be the whole focus of my life. I need another way to get more distance from what happened so I can move on with my life.

Carla wrote this description of a painful experience in her Recognizing a River You Have Crossed exercise:

I guess the hardest thing I ever went through was being sexually abused by Grandpa. It made me feel like a nothing. Sometimes when it was happening I just wanted to die.

1. (What did you learn from surviving this experience?)
   Surviving it, at first while it was going on, meant that I had to find things to take my mind off it. I remember as a kid practicing the cello for hours, anything to get away from the horrible feelings I had when I would think about what Grandpa was doing to me. I couldn't make him stop because he was a very violent man, and I was afraid of how he would retaliate if I told on him.

2. (What strengths or talents did you draw on then or develop later to survive the experience?)
   I remember seeing the movie *Chorus Line* and this woman in the movie talking about how much she liked practicing ballet because there (at the ballet) everything was beautiful and okay. That's how it was for me with the cello, and that was a talent I developed in order to cope. Later I got stronger, and in groups I learned how to express my feelings and how to get angry when I needed to and how to stand up for myself.

   Being able to stand up for myself and get angry when it is appropriate was especially important because it was something I could never do when I was being abused. It is a strength I developed later, after the abuse, in order to survive the fact that it had happened to me, and to protect myself from other kinds of abuse. Being able to get angry has helped me stop people from trying to abuse me emotionally or financially.

3. (How can these strengths or talents be used to your best advantage now?) As far as using these skills [standing up for myself and playing the cello] to my best advantage in my life right now, I think maybe it's time for me to start playing music again. I haven't played the cello for five or six years. I don't even have one anymore, but I still like listening to music. I want to start spending more time with music, listening to some CDs, maybe going to some concerts. I think I might like to learn a new instrument, one that is more portable, maybe the guitar. As far as standing up for myself, I want to become more assertive at work.

If you have not already done so, take a moment to do the Recognizing a River You Have Crossed exercise at the beginning of this section.

Harvesting Your Past
This chapter's final exercise will integrate the work you did in the previous exercises while you further harvest the knowledge and resources you developed in order to survive the past. As with the other exercises in this book, you may record your responses on paper or on audiotape. And you can repeat the exercise as often as you wish.

 One Small Step
Take a few minutes to daydream about your life in the future. Imagine that you are productively using all the knowledge you have gleaned from both past experiences that you would prefer to forget and those you want to remember.

Everything you have learned is part of your personal wisdom. You don't have to grow old to acquire wisdom, only to have lived truly and fully.

While this chapter has focused on ways to address and resolve the lingering effects of the past, the next chapter will offer help for coping and finding comfort on those stressful days and nights that sometimes occur in your present life.

CHAPTER NINE

DEALING WITH RAINY DAYS
AND DARK NIGHTS

*...This morning I woke at four and lay awake for an hour or so in a bad state.
It is raining again. I got up finally and went about the daily chores, waiting
for the sense of doom to lift—and what did it was watering the houseplants.
Suddenly joy came back because I was fulfilling a simple need, a living one.*

—May Sarton

*Sometimes I found that in my happy moments I could not believe
that I had ever been miserable....While in my moments of despair
I could not even remember what happiness felt like.*

—Joanna Field

Is there anyone in the world who has reached adulthood and never had an emotionally
dark period, the sort we sometimes refer to euphemistically as rainy days and dark
nights? I doubt it.

I have been no stranger to dark days. Divorce, illnesses, deaths of people I love, and
other losses have all triggered rainy days.

This chapter offers a variety of methods for coping with your dark nights and rainy
days when you experience them, as well as ways to prepare for future gloomy moments.
The first section reminds you that maintaining your health can lessen the impact of
personal troubles. The next section describes ways you can express and thereby release
some of your stressful feelings. The third section helps you update your expectations
for yourself. And the final section prepares you for those inevitable rainy days.

Experiencing occasional despondency is not a sign of failure in your efforts to be
true to your Authentic Self and to create a joyous life. Most people feel dejected now
and then. Such dreary times are less troubling if you think of them as what they are;

transitory rather than permanent states that gradually pass as you go about the business of daily life. Experiencing contrasting emotional states is part of living wholly and soulfully.

I want to emphasize that the emotional states I am talking about in this chapter are not episodes of severe clinical depression. While darker days may evoke uncomfortable feelings of restlessness, anger, confusion, sadness, or anxiety, they are by definition not life threatening. If at any time you experience numerous consecutive days of depression without relief, or if you experience suicidal thoughts, seek professional help.

TAKING CARE OF YOURSELF

As a psychotherapist I've found that most people forget about the basics when they are upset and need them the most. So to begin at the beginning, maintaining your physical health is an important aspect of maintaining your emotional well-being.

Eat a Decent Meal

When you have a bad day or night, check to make sure that you have eaten. Many people forget to eat or eat poorly when they are upset. If you have a tendency toward hypoglycemia (low blood sugar), the lack of food in your system will worsen your feelings of depression and anxiety.

Loading up on caffeine and sugar rather than healthy food can also contribute negatively to the intensity of your feelings. This is also true of alcohol. So make sure that your strategy for coping with a difficult time includes a healthy meal or snack. Your grandmother was right, eating something good for you can make you feel better.

Get Some Rest

How much sleep have you had? Exhaustion may be contributing to your gloomy period. Like food, sleep or the lack of it effects the intensity of emotions, particularly negative ones. If you don't believe me, remember a time you spent in the company of a cranky young child who missed his nap.

Sleep deprivation affects adults, too. Having struggled with workaholic tendencies, I used to mistake my state of exhaustion for depression. Eventually I realized that what I thought was a bad day was usually a day when I was trying to do too much in too short a time when I had slept too little the night before.

Take a Bath

There is an anonymous saying that was popular in our grandparents' era: There are few problems that cannot be improved by a hot bath and a good night's sleep. It's still true. A warm, peaceful bath may help soothe your tenseness and give you the serenity to work through the day's anxieties.

Take a Break

Remember your Ultradian rhythms I talked about in Chapter Six? People function best if they take a break every hour and a half to two hours. Ignoring your body's need for these breaks can result in increased stress, difficulty concentrating, and a higher risk for illness. Take a twenty-minute break and notice the difference it makes.

Exercise

Do you feel sluggish? Is your body tense? How much exercise have you been getting? A brisk walk or an aerobic workout does a lot more than just tone your body. It will clear your mind and calm your thoughts, improving your likelihood of sleeping well. Exercise also stimulates the production of endorphins, the body's natural antidepressant.

If you feel you don't have enough time to work out regularly, you are probably experiencing a stress level that necessitates you do so! So shelve your other obligations for an hour and get some exercise. You'll get more done afterward with your increased energy. Believe me, I know, because I learned the hard way. I used to be the queen of the sedentary lifestyle.

Get a Massage

Are your neck and shoulders tight? Is your stomach churning? Have you been under pressure at home, at work, in life? If so, your body is probably talking to you, maybe even yelling at you in an attempt to get your attention so you'll slow down and relax. Set up an appointment for a massage, or if you're lucky enough to have a friend or family member who gives a good back rub, arrange time for one. If you need a massage, you deserve one.

Give Yourself a Foot Rub

Perhaps there's no one available to give you a massage right now. Massage your own feet instead and notice the resulting feelings of relaxation and well-being as you knead, rub, and soothe those hardworking muscles. Begin by soaking your feet in a tub of warm salt water, drying them, and rubbing them with a scented foot lotions. Then work progressively over the upper and lower surface of each foot, using small circular movements of your thumbs and fingers. You may have forgotten anything could feel so good!

Get a Medical Checkup

Are you experiencing physical distress? Has it been going on for a while? If your blues are accompanied by consistent physical symptoms, there may be a medical cause. I once found myself in a state of anxiety and frustration because I couldn't seem to carry out my normal obligations and routines even though I was eating right and getting enough sleep. It was only when I visited my doctor for my yearly checkup that I discovered I had mononucleosis, a virus associated with fatigue.

LISTEN TO YOURSELF

Rainy days and dark nights sometimes provide the gift of reassessing your values and beliefs. Sometimes the best way to receive this gift is to acknowledge what you are feeling and listen to your soul's response. Writing about what you are experiencing is a good way to do this. Expressing your feelings in writing can provide release and enough psychological distance to accurately assess the circumstances, event, or situation that evoked the feelings. What are you trying to tell yourself?

As a survivor of sexual abuse, I had a dark night of despair several years ago when the price of my telling the truth resulted in rejection and estrangement from some people who wanted to protect the abusers at any price. This excerpt from my journal at that time illustrates how the discouraging experience also contained the seed for my moving beyond the darkness:

With great sadness last night, I heard their words, "You are losing your relationship with us [by refusing to lie for us]." I was very disappointed in their lack of integrity in asking me to lie, but I was even more heartbroken by the fact that I had lost my own illusion of goodness about them. In a sense I had lost the people I thought they were, and that loss was irretrievable.

After I had sat crying for a while, a thought came to me, and it is one that I don't ever want to forget: "Yes, you have lost them, but you get to be true to yourself for the rest of your life." I realized that while it can be terrible to lose someone or something you love, it is worse to lose your integrity, that is, your Authentic Self. I immediately felt a sense of calm, the seed of which grew to joy a few hours later when I looked out my window and saw the moonlight shining on our old apple trees.

Remember Other Rainy Days
What gift have you received from past rainy days and dark nights? Sit quietly and answer the following questions.

 One Small Step
Think back to dark days you have had in the past.

 Possibilities
- What were they like?
- What things, people or actions, triggered your bad feelings?
- What did you do, or what helped you eventually shift out of the dark period?
- How might you apply this to a current situation in your life right now?

Consider a Personal Ritual
If your dark period is characterized by intrusive and upsetting thoughts or images from the past, try the Write, Read, and Burn; Drawing Relief; or Rewriting Negative Messages exercises from Chapter Eight.

Declare a "Snow Day"

How long has it been since you've had any time for yourself, away from the outside world? In Northern Michigan where I grew up, winter was a long season. Fortunately the grey snow cloud-filled skies brought the gift of "snow days," unplanned holidays that came when it was too stormy to leave the house. On these days you could do whatever you wanted—either catch up on chores or just enjoy yourself around the house. After spending too much time in large crowds of people, a snow day may be just what you need.

Get Out of the House

Did you cringe when I suggested a snow day? Maybe staying indoors is just more of what you have been doing and is the last thing you want when you have the blues. If so, get outside or go somewhere different than your usual environment.

If the weather is bad, consider walking through indoor botanical gardens, a museum, or even a shopping mall.

Don't Just Sit There, Pound a Pillow!

No, I'm not kidding. Are you angry about something? Sometimes depression or anxiety is the result of anger turned inward. Anger is energy, and discharging it can make you feel better. If pounding a pillow feels too ridiculous, start by expressing your negative feelings in writing and then consider doing some form of physical work as a release.

Leaf raking, snow shoveling, and spading a flower bed are all good physical releases. So are scrubbing floors and washing windows, or sanding the paint off an old piece of furniture. Any activity requiring a lot of elbow grease can expel some of your anger. Afterward you'll feel better, and you'll have accomplished something worthwhile.

Call a Friend

Melancholy thrives on isolation and so does full-blown depression! Ironically, we sometimes choose to be alone when it is the worst thing for us. There are two kinds of support a friend can lend when you're feeling down. The first is listening to your troubles, and the second is getting your mind off them by talking about other things. Both types of help are valuable. Since most friends are better at one of these than the other, call whichever friend best suits your current needs.

Reconnect to Your Hopes and Dreams

Have you forgotten your cherished hopes and daydreams, or perhaps they seem far away right now. If so, why not take some time to do the Letter from the Future exercise in Chapter Four?

Reconnect to the Present

If your dark night or rainy day is connected to feelings about the past, you may need to mentally reconnect to the present. That way you can assess and deal with your feelings with the resources of an adult perspective.

 One Small Step

Take a moment to think about what you reminds you of who you are now. What is different about your environment from where you lived in the past? Take a look around you and note the colors, shapes, sounds, and textures surrounding you.

Imagine what advice you would give to another person who came to you with the problem or feelings with which you are currently contending.

Make Your Favorite Comfort Food

Did you have a favorite food as a child? Mine was plain old macaroni with a simple homemade tomato sauce. These days I gussy it up a little with basil and garlic and a sprinkling of freshly grated Parmesan cheese, but it still evokes the same feelings of well-being as when I was a kid. What foods bring comfort to you? Indulged in moderation, they will do no harm, and just may help you feel better.

Plan a Vacation

Sometimes escapism is just what's needed even if you can't go on a vacation immediately. Instead, spend a few minutes imagining your planned vacation—where you will go, what you will do, and how joyful and relaxed you will feel. Just knowing that a vacation is in your future can relieve stress as you enjoy temporarily fantasizing about it.

Lose Yourself in Great Music

In the winter my husband and I ritually sit by the fireplace and listen to music for an hour or more every night after dinner. Sometimes we read or I quilt while listening, and other times we just allow the music to soothe us, letting our thoughts drift and our bodies melt into the relaxation that can come from being absorbed in beautiful harmonies. While music is oftentimes a pleasant background for conversations, work, and activities, it offers a significant release when listened to while doing nothing.

Enjoy Armchair Travel

Go to the library or bookstore and get yourself a book or video that describes a place you've always wanted to visit. You can "go away" to somewhere exotic for several hours for next to nothing this way, and you will emerge refreshed and relaxed.

Give Yourself a Spa Day

Many health clubs and beauty salons offer day spas during which you can bask during a combination of beauty treatments and a relaxing massage. If you can't afford a professional treatment, arrange to give yourself one at home.

Plan a Garden

Do you like gardens? Seed catalogs are usually free and are illustrated with beautiful flowers, trees, and shrubs. Just paging through one invites the fantasy of a dream garden. Why not indulge in planning your own dream garden, and begin a wish list of plants you plan to buy when you have the time, money, or yard.

Learn Something New

When is the last time you did something just for the fun of it? Is it time to start a new hobby or develop a new interest? Language classes, crafts, and taking up a new sport are just a few of the ways you can bring a new spark to your life.

Pray

A friend told me about a wonderful saying she learned in Alcoholics Anonymous, "Let go, and let God." If you believe in God or another higher power, praying about whatever is distressing you and turning it over to Him or Her or whoever you imagine God to be can make a big difference. When I am troubled, regardless of whether I am in my hometown or far away in a foreign country, I go into a church, light a candle, and pray. It always helps me.

Help Someone Less Fortunate Than Yourself

After my grandmother died several years ago following a long illness, I found myself feeling emotionally depleted. The world around me seemed bleak without her presence, and my normal grief process seemed in danger of disintegrating into narcissistic self-pity. I began volunteering at a shelter for homeless women, and my perspective shifted quickly.

The possibilities for volunteer work are unlimited. There are Big Sisters, Big Brothers organizations to help disadvantaged youth, homeless shelters, Meals on Wheels, the Red Cross, and many more. Helping doesn't need to be limited to helping other humans. If you are an animal lover, why not volunteer at your local Humane Society or Dumb Friends League, or better yet adopt a homeless pet. All of our pets were originally strays, and I know from experience that they will return the love and care you give them with undying loyalty and affection.

Perhaps you don't need to look as far as charitable organizations to find an outlet for your desire to help. Is there a friend, a relative, or a neighbor near you who could benefit from your support and kindness? Don't overlook the needs of adolescents and children, as along with the elderly, they are among our most vulnerable citizens.

CLEARING AWAY YOUR OUTDATED EXPECTATIONS

Sometimes rainy days come because you're mistakenly trying to be someone you were in the past, but no longer are. When I was younger and had more time and knew fewer people, I made all my own Christmas presents and baked homemade treats for everyone I cared about. The Christmas season was always a joyous time for me.

That was until a few years ago when I found myself collapsed in bed with the flu in mid-December as I frantically tried to figure out how I was going to bake all those cookies and finish all those half-completed gifts for family and friends. The truth was hard to face.

I couldn't do it all. In fact I probably had gotten sick as a result of trying to produce all those homespun, heartfelt gifts and treats while shouldering a heavy workload in my professional life! Once I realized that I was no longer the free spirit I had once been before my workload and relationships became extensive, my holidays became serene again. I still give people homemade treats, but I often purchase them at the local church bazaar. And I'm able to enjoy the holidays again.

Take a moment now to review your current expectations of yourself. Do they need to be updated to reflect the realities of the life you now live?

For example, are you trying to keep your home as clean as you did when you had fewer responsibilities or were the only one living there? If so, maybe you need to reevaluate your standards or enlist the help of the other people who live with you. Or if you can afford it, why not hire a cleaning service? If you are trying to do too much in other areas of your life, consider reordering your priorities.

Figure Out Who You Are Apart from Your "Shoulds"
Spending our time doing what we believe we "should" be doing or ought to be doing can not only be unsatisfying, but can deprive us of the joy we deserve from life.

 One Small Step
If left unfettered, but nurtured and supported, how would you choose to pass your time? Notice what thoughts and images come to mind as you imagine this.

 Possibilities
- If you lived more in accord with your envisioned preferences rather than spending so much time on what you "should" do, what productive or useful things might occur in your life?
- What is one small step you could take to initiate some of these newly discovered activities?
- What small sign would show that you had begun to move in this direction?

Mend an Emotional Fence

My great-grandmother, who was deservedly famous for her Irish temper, got mad at a close friend over a minor slight. Although the friend lived just down the street, they didn't speak to each other for the next twenty years.

Finally, bursting with a piece of irresistible news (her daughter had given birth to twins) my great-grandmother broke the ice and spoke to her friend. They immediately resumed their relationship as if nothing had happened. In the meantime they had missed out on twenty years of good times they could have shared. My great-grandmother must have felt sad during all those years when she walked past her estranged friend's house.

Consider reaching out to an estranged friend. Or, if you are feeling the pain of a deep emotional wound in a significant relationship, do the Healing Letters exercise in Chapter Eight.

Possibilities
- Are you holding a grudge against someone you really care about?
- What is one small step you could take to repair your friendship?

Life is too short to carry the heavy burden of extended suffering from painful past relationships.

Check Your Personal Boundaries

Are you overwhelmed by duties or responsibilities that should not rightfully be yours? Is someone exploiting you by making unreasonable demands on your time and energy? If so, the dark night or rainy day you are experiencing may be an indication that it is time to set limits with that person, to draw a boundary around your availability to them.

With the exception of dependent children and adults unable to care for themselves, people are individually responsible for themselves. Consistently doing for others what they need to do for themselves, or repeatedly rescuing them from the consequences of irresponsibility will accomplish little other than wearing you out. And it can prevent them from taking the necessary actions to move forward in their life.

Possibilities
- Are people's expectations infringing on your life?
- If so, what is one small change you could make to modify this situation?

Reorganize Your Home

As a psychotherapist I have noticed an interesting phenomenon over the years, especially among women. After reorganizing their home, people often realize in retrospect that they were simultaneously reorganizing their mental priorities and shifting their psychological perspectives. When you have the time, rearrange the areas in your home to suit your current lifestyle.

Possibilities
- What did you discover about the changes in your life when you reorganized your home?

For a more extended discussion of making your home environment reflect and nurture you, see Chapter Two.

PREPARING FOR FUTURE RAINY DAYS AND DARK NIGHTS

While we can't always predict a difficult day or evening in advance, creating a Rainy Day Comfort Box and writing a Rainy Day Letter can help us prepare for difficult times and make their occurrence less upsetting.

The Rainy Day Comfort Box

In *Simple Abundance*, Sarah Ban Breathnach suggests outfitting a "comfort drawer" to have ready when you need it. Opening a Rainy Day Comfort Box on a gloomy day and visiting your fondest keepsakes can restore the light and beauty to your day.

What nourishes your mind and spirit? Do you have a favorite herb tea, a special bubble bath scent, a candle, or incense that soothes you? Books on aromatherapy offer suggestions for scents that help induce relaxation, reinvigorate, or invite sleep. Some companies offer herbal bath products labeled according to their aromatic purpose.

You might include special letters, cards, or photographs that evoke happy memories. A favorite book of poems or a collection of cartoons and jokes you've clipped out of newspapers and magazines would work. A soft silk pillow for your eyes (available at health food stores and some gift shops) is an idea. You might want to include a teddy bear or stuffed animal; they comfort many adults as well as children. You can find additional ideas in *The Woman's Comfort Book* by Jennifer Louden, a book you may want to keep in your Rainy Day Comfort Box.

 One Small Step
Line a box or drawer with pretty wrapping paper or cloth in a pattern that delights you. Then put the things you have collected inside.

The Rainy Day Letter

Sometimes you can see a rainy day approaching on the horizon: a dear friend's terminal illness, the inevitable pain of imminent divorce proceedings, the bittersweet transition of a much-loved child leaving for college. Other times dark periods come with no warning. In either case, these difficult times can be eased by preparing for them in advance with a Rainy Day Letter.

The Rainy Day Letter is the psychological version of the Rainy Day Comfort Box. Ironically, when we most need comfort is when it's most difficult to remember or figure out what would help. The Rainy Day Letter will provide personal consolation when you most need it. Since a letter is more portable than a box, you can carry it with you to support you wherever you are. And it offers the wisdom of the person who knows you best: yourself!

 One Small Step
Set aside some time when you are calm and can relate this serenity to yourself at a future time when you are upset, overwhelmed, or distressed. Write this letter from you, to you.

1. List activities that you find comforting.
2. Record the names and phone numbers of supportive friends or family members.

3. Remind yourself of your strengths and virtues.
4. Remind yourself of your special talents, abilities, and interests.
5. Remind yourself of some of your hopes and dreams for the future.
6. Give yourself special advice or other reminders that are important to you.

Here is a portion of a Rainy Day Letter I wrote for myself several years ago. It is not intended as an ideal example of what your letter should look like, but as an illustration to help get you started in creating your own.

Dear Yvonne,

When you read this in the future, you will probably be feeling down on your luck, saddened, weary, upset about something. Whatever you are feeling right now, this letter is for you.

Find a comfortable place to sit down while you read it. Would it help to make yourself a cup of chamomile tea first so you can sip it as you read? I know tea warms your spirit.

If you are feeling down on yourself right now, I want to remind you that while you are not perfect you do have some good character traits: you tend to finish what you start, you try hard to be fair and loyal in your relationships, and you have a good sense of humor.

Have you eaten? Why not make yourself macaroni with tomato sauce?

Have you been sleeping okay? If not, how about a hot bath and a nap?

What about exercise? Maybe you need to get outdoors. Maybe it would help to take a walk in the woods. Or if you're far from home, why don't you go into a church and pray? That always helps you.

Would it help to call a friend? Maybe you need to talk to Charlie, your husband and best friend of all. Or maybe you need to talk to another woman. You could call ____ or _____ or _____ (phone numbers).

Or maybe you're emotionally drained, worried about something you can't control. If so, why not shut the door and turn off the phone. Watch one of those vintage black-and-white movies from the '40s that you love, or reread your favorite passages from Pablo Neruda's *Odes to Opposites.*

The bottom line here, my dear, is that it's okay, in fact it's important to take some time right now to figure out what you need to do in order to feel better, and then do it. And remember, whatever it is, this too will pass. Whatever else happens, I will always be here for you, because I am you.

Love,
Me

If you haven't already, take some time now to begin your Rainy Day Letter. You deserve the comfort it will bring. Rereading it and implementing some of the ideas in your letter really can make a difference in times of stress and distress. I know this not only from personal experience but from hundreds of people I have seen in my psychotherapy practice and in my workshops.

Finally, remember that nothing, be it a bad day or night or an upsetting event, will go on forever. Change is inevitable, and sooner or later this too will pass.

This chapter has offered a variety of things you can do to cope with, learn from, and get past difficult times and prepare for the ones that come in the future. The next chapter will provide suggestions, guidelines, and a format for creating the nurturing and exhilarating environment of a Small Steps Support Group based on the exercises in this book.

PART FOUR

SUPPORT AND
FURTHER RESOURCES

CHAPTER TEN

HOW TO START A SMALL STEPS SUPPORT GROUP

The only true gift is a portion of yourself.

—Ralph Waldo Emerson

Telling one's troubles to a supportive listener undoes the isolation that often worsens pain. You no longer feel alone in trying to cope with your problem.

Similarly, telling a sympathetic person your hopes, dreams, and plans strengthens your ability to take action and make these things happen. Talking about a goal can make it seem more real and more achievable. Furthermore, once you have talked to another person about a cherished hope or dream, it is harder to dismiss its importance, forget about it, or otherwise lose track of it. A group of supportive people can be invaluable in helping each other identify and then gradually complete the small progressive steps that are part of achieving any goal. Small Steps Support Groups are designed to provide such mutual aid while fostering each member's continued exploration and creative expression of her Authentic Self.

The first four sections of this chapter provide practical information and guidelines for structuring, starting, and ending a Small Steps Support Group. The next section offers basic questions to be used in the group, and the final section is comprised of a collection of exercises that have been adapted for Small Steps Support Groups.

THE GROUP STRUCTURE

The organizers should begin by deciding when, where, and for how many sessions the group will meet and who will lead the sessions.

You can start a group on your own by inviting several supportive friends, or you can enlist the help of a professional psychotherapist or counselor to organize and conduct the group. If you employ a professional, be sure they have been trained in Solution-focused therapy and have had prior experience leading groups.

It is best to start with a time-limited group, such as scheduling four to six sessions, with the provision that at the last session group members can elect to continue for another specified period. An initial commitment for longer than six sessions may be daunting for some people and prevent them from joining the group.

Group sessions usually vary from an hour and a half to two hours depending on the size of the group. I suggest that a group have at least three people, but no more than ten. It is imperative that each member get a chance to talk, and this becomes difficult if a group is too large.

If there is not an official designated leader for the group, members should arrange to rotate leadership among them, agreeing in advance how this will be done. The leader is responsible for ensuring that each person has an opportunity to answer the Basic Group Questions and for selecting one of the group exercises from this chapter.

Setting a kitchen timer is one way to ensure that everyone has a chance to speak. I recommend allowing no more than five minutes for each member until everyone has had a chance to answer the first three Basic Group Questions. Some groups will naturally share time more or less equally.

GENERAL GUIDELINES

As a basic ground rule, group members should agree that their role with one another is to be nurturing and validating. The purpose of the group is to provide psychological support and encouragement for people who want to explore their hopes and dreams and actively pursue the series of gradual small steps that will allow them to overcome obstacles and achieve the life they want and deserve.

Criticism or amateur psychoanalysis of one another's shortcomings are *not* part of a Small Steps Support Group. Information shared by a member during a meeting is to be kept confidential, and should not be shared or discussed outside the group without that person's permission. The only exception is a situation in which someone is in life-threatening danger.

THE MECHANICS OF A SMALL STEPS SUPPORT GROUP

The first meeting should begin with each member introducing herself and then answering the following questions:

Possibilities
- What would you like to have happen as a result of attending this group?
- What are some of the goals, hopes, and dreams for which you want support and encouragement from the other group members?
- Of these, what goal would you like to begin with?

Whether a Small Steps Support Group elects to meet for just a few weeks or becomes an ongoing group that meets for months or even years, the Basic Group Questions are a good way to keep meetings on track and help members acknowledge and support one another's continued growth and progress.

After the first meeting, subsequent meetings are comprised of answering the Basic Group Questions and completing one exercise listed in the following section. For example, depending on the size of the group, a ninety-minute meeting might be divided into two forty-minute segments with a ten-minute break in between. The first half of the meeting could be devoted to the members answering the Basic Group Questions, and the second half would focus on group members completing and discussing that week's exercise. On occasions when the group undertakes a longer exercise, such as the Time Line or the two-part Creating a New Influence exercise, the group might decide to begin the exercise during their meeting and complete it at home, discussing it in a subsequent meeting.

The final section of this chapter is comprised of written instructions for the Basic Group Questions and the exercises from *One Small Step* best suited to a group format. Having spent over three thousand hours leading various groups, I have learned from experience that giving participants individual written instructions simplifies things. For convenience I have listed the questions and exercises on individual pages so they can be photocopied and distributed to group members. Repeatedly using the combination of the Basic Group Questions and the exercises in this chapter will help establish a climate of safety and trust in the group that enables people to identify with and enact the small steps that lead to the fulfillment of their hopes and dreams.

ENDING THE GROUP

As the final session of your Small Steps Support Group approaches, invite members to reflect on and tell one another what the group has meant to them and what they have learned from other group members. The Rainy Day Letter from the Group exercise at the end of this chapter can be used when a group is ending or when a member is leaving.

BASIC GROUP QUESTIONS

1. What aspects of your goal have stayed the same, worsened, or improved since the last group meeting?
2. How did the improvements happen?
3. How could you continue the improvement or even make it happen more often?

If a group member reports that nothing is better, and is discouraged or disgruntled, invite them to answer the next three questions:

4. Does the goal you are working on feel too overwhelming or too large? If yes, proceed to question 5. If no, skip question 5.
5. On a scale of 1 to 10—10 means you have achieved your goal, and 1 means you haven't even thought about your goal—where are you now? What would raise your score a half point? What would raise it a whole point? Is this something you want to try? If no or unsure, proceed to the following questions.
6. How is it that things are not worse? What useful things have you or others done to prevent things from getting worse?
7. Is there any advantage, even a small one, to things not getting better for you? If so, how might you manage to preserve some of this advantage while moving forward on improving things?
8. If after the above questions a group member is still feeling stuck or discouraged, proceed to the Miracle Question at the beginning of the Selected Group Exercises.

In all cases it is crucial that these questions be offered and received in a supportive, noncritical, and respectful spirit, and be based upon a sincere desire to help yourself and your fellow group members. If in responding to the Basic Questions, someone becomes sidetracked or has trouble answering, she can ask the group for help and support, or progress to the Miracle Question in the next section of this chapter.

THE MIRACLE QUESTION

Imagine that in the middle of the night, while you were asleep, a miracle happened and you had achieved the hopes, goals, or dreams that brought you to this group.

Possibilities
- What would be different when you awakened?
- What would be the first small change in your behavior that you would notice?
- What would the people who live with you notice?
- What would the people who work with you notice?
- What changes in your behavior—indicating that this miracle had happened since the last time they saw you—would the other members of your Small Steps Support Group observe at your next meeting?

One Small Step
Choose one small behavioral change that would represent a step toward your miracle and practice doing it between now and the next group meeting. Report the results to the group.

If you have trouble coming up with small signs that your miracle has happened, try this: Imagine that you have a videotape of yourself that started running the moment your miracle happened in the middle of the night. What would you notice yourself doing if you were watching the videotape of yourself the first day (and night) after your miracle had happened? What would be the first image or frame on the videotape that would indicate to you that your miracle had happened? What would be the next one?

This exercise can be especially useful when you are feeling stuck or dispirited about a problem. It will help clarify how your hopes or goals might transpire in real life, and help you identify the small steps necessary to move toward achieving them.

A MESSAGE FROM A GUARDIAN ANGEL

Imagine that a wise and compassionate guardian angel has been sitting on your shoulder since you were born. You have not been aware of this presence up until now because angels are weightless. The angel's sole purpose has been to recognize and observe all of your positive personality strengths and virtuous beliefs about the world. This is not an angel in charge of producing self-criticism or blame!

 One Small Step
For the next fifteen minutes, imagine that the angel is now dictating a list of your positive attributes through you. Writing down whatever comes to mind, make a list of what you think the angel would say.

Possibilities
- Which personality traits do you value most and want to continue to influence your approach to life?
- Which virtues or positive beliefs do you value most and want to continue to influence your approach to life?

Once you have completed this exercise, take some time to contemplate what you wrote.

This exercise is helpful for reclaiming and bolstering your self-confidence and courage.

A LETTER FROM THE FUTURE

One Small Step

Pick a time in the future (five, ten, fifteen, twenty years from now or any other length of time that is meaningful to you). Record the future date you have chosen at the head of your letter. Imagine that the intervening years have passed and you are writing to a friend. Choose someone you know and with whom you would like to continue to be friends in the future. Use the friend's name in the salutation, as in Dear (friend's name).

When writing the letter, imagine that you are living a joyous, healthy, satisfying life by the letter's date. If there are problems with which you are now struggling, assume that they have either been resolved or that you have found satisfying ways to cope with them by the time of the letter.

Explain how you resolved problems or difficulties that once plagued you. Tell what you found to be most helpful from the vantage point of looking back on your current life from the future.

Describe in detail how you spend your time in this imaginary future. What is a typical day? Where are you living? Describe your relationships, beliefs, reflections on the past, and speculations toward the more distant future.

This letter is not meant to be mailed. It is for you only. The purpose of dating the letter and writing it to a real person is to strengthen the psychological realism of the letter for you on both conscious and unconscious levels.

In writing your letter, don't worry about limiting yourself to things that seem realistic given your current life. This is not essential and may constrict you unnecessarily. Your Letter from the Future should be written with an open heart and an open mind so you have room to surprise yourself.

CREATING A SYMBOL TO CENTER YOURSELF

 Possibilities
- When in your life have you felt most relaxed, calm and centered? Select one experience you would enjoy remembering again in the future.
- What was it about this experience that you found most relaxing and meaningful? Notice what images, thoughts, or words come to mind.

 One Small Step
Now draw a picture or choose an object, photograph, or quotation that reminds you of that experience and that you can carry with you in the future.

Use this symbol to center, calm, and replenish yourself when life becomes stressful or when you simply want to relax.

THE HEART'S DESIRE COLLAGE

The Heart's Desire Collage will amplify your hopes and dreams. Giving them a tangible representation will also strengthen their presence in your unconscious.

Collect symbolic items ahead of time by assembling some photos, postcards, drawings, or images from magazines that remind you of your heart's desires. Pieces of paper, leather, or fabric in your favorite colors are also appropriate because they can evoke the positive feelings you associate with various shades and textures. You may also want to include objects from nature such as twigs, dried flowers, or small shells. Don't forget any work you have drawn yourself. You can also write words directly on your collage.

One Small Step

Set aside at least an hour for this exercise. Where you spend this time is important. Make sure you have privacy or, if there are people around, they should be nonjudgmental and supportive of what you are doing. You will need a piece of cardboard or heavy paper at least 8 by 10 inches, scissors, glue, writing or drawing implements, and a collection of things that symbolize the hopes and dreams you began to explore in your Letter from the Future.

Now glue your collected objects onto the piece of cardboard or paper. Arrange things in any pattern that pleases you. You can overlap or layer items, create a picture, or randomly paste things into a design that abstractly expresses your heart's desire for your future.

When making your collage, remember that the goal is to rediscover the free and childlike imagination of you Authentic Self. That means you are allowed to be playful and spontaneous, and it's fine to be messy. Don't be surprised if additional ideas occur to you while you're in the middle of making the collage.

This exercise is helpful for further exploring your hopes and dreams and making them more present in your daily awareness.

THE LAST FIFTEEN MINUTES OF THE WORLD

For this exercise you will need some blank paper and writing or drawing implements.

Imagine that you have been gifted at birth with two things: the ability to express yourself well and some special knowledge to give the world. Unfortunately, you have not known of these abilities until now. You have also just learned that a terrible destructive force is about to hit the earth. This destructive force will destroy all libraries, museums, computers, and other information storage systems. Only those objects and information placed in a special time capsule will survive.

 One Small Step

You are asked to contribute to the time capsule. Write, draw, or orally record your special information to help the human race survive after the catastrophe. You have only fifteen minutes to do this.

Identifying ideas or thoughts deep within that you deem meaningful and important allows you to appreciate your unique knowledge and reflect it more fully in your daily life.

CREATING A NEW INFLUENCE FOR YOUR LIFE

 One Small Step
Think of someone who embodies a way of living that you value, a person you admire in some way. This person can be living or dead, famous or unknown. He or she can be someone you know personally, or someone you are acquainted with only through literature, movies, or stories you have heard. If at all possible, find a picture of this person (or draw one) to look at while doing this exercise.

Write a detailed description of this person, emphasizing the qualities that you most admire.

Think about why you have chosen him or her to be an influence in your life.

 Possibilities
• What do you find most appealing about this person's approach to life?
• How would this person respond to your current situation?

Now that you have completed your Creating a New Influence exercise, the following questions will help you further integrate the positive qualities you identified into your own personality.

 One Small Step
Think back to the person you chose as a new influence for your life.

 Possibilities
• How are you like the person you described in the Creating a New Influence exercise?
• How are you different?
• What aspects of this person's lifestyle do you wish to incorporate into your life?

• Are there any things that you are already doing that are examples of this?
  If so, what would be the effect of doing a little more of this in order to integrate this quality further into your personality? If not, what would be the
  first small step toward embodying their way of living?

If you don't believe you possess any of your chosen person's admirable qualities,
what would be a small observable sign in your behavior that showed you were beginning
to incorporate such qualities? Consider a scale of 1 to 10 in which 10 meant you had
succeeded in incorporating a newly desired quality into your behavior to the fullest
degree possible, and 1 meant not at all.

What observable practice could you undertake that would raise your score a half
point or more? Experiment with enacting the behavior you identified, noticing the difference doing it makes for you. Then identify the next small step that would develop
the desired quality and try that, and so on. Report the results to the group.

A TREE THAT SPEAKS TO YOU

This exercise needs to be done at a time of year when the group can walk around outdoors in a wooded setting. The tree is a device upon which you can project your
thoughts, feelings, and special awareness, thereby allowing your Authentic Self to speak
to you.

 One Small Step
Give yourself a minimum of an hour to walk around and contemplate various
trees. Look for a tree that you find particularly appealing. Imagine that this
tree has something to tell you about your Authentic Self. Imagine that the tree
knows something important about you because you are kindred spirits. Ask
the tree to tell you how you are alike, and write down what comes to mind.
Then ask the tree to tell you the message it has for you about your Authentic
Self, and write down whatever you imagine the tree tells you.

Identifying with nature is another avenue for getting more deeply in touch with your
Authentic Self.

A TIME LINE—YOUR LIFE STORY

You will need paper and pencil.

One Small Step
Draw a vertical line down the middle of a sheet of paper. On the upper
left-hand corner write the word *birth* and your date of birth. Now list other
demographic information about yourself such as approximate dates of starting
school, moves, birth(s) of siblings, and so on in chronological order. Add
information as it comes to you, including both pleasant and unpleasant information that you deem significant.

Record past or current feelings about each event in the space across from it
on the right-hand side of the vertical line.

One page will probably not be enough. You may think of additional information
that needs to be inserted to a retain a chronological order to your Time Line. Just cut
the paper horizontally and tape together additional strips of paper to insert new text.
You may continue using paper and tape to form one long strip of paper that you can
roll up and store in the form of a long scroll.

Discovering and exploring your life story is another way to deepen a connection
with your Authentic Self.

A COAT OF ARMS

If you were to create a Coat of Arms to represent your Authentic Self what images would you include? What colors best represent who you are? Would you include things that represent your accomplishments, your hobbies and other things you like to do? Is there a saying or a logo that you would include in the form of an inscription or a banner? Notice what comes to mind.

You will need blank paper; drawing, coloring, or painting supplies; glue; and some old magazines or newspapers for this exercise.

 One Small Step
Draw a Coat of Arms for yourself on a sheet of paper and notice what emerges. Feel free to add images cut out from newspapers and magazines, as well as objects from nature such as discarded feathers, bits of dried wood, or flowers. Remember that the idea in creating a Coat of Arms is to learn more about your Authentic Self. Don't worry if your creation is not great art!

This exercise will help you strengthen your self-confidence and a positive self-identity.

A RAINY DAY LETTER

Ironically, when we most need comfort is when it's most difficult to remember or figure out what would help. The Rainy Day Letter will provide consolation when you most need it. Since a letter is portable, you can carry it with you to support you wherever you are. And it offers the wisdom of the person who knows you best: yourself!

 One Small Step
Set aside some time when you are calm and can relate this serenity to yourself at a future time when you are upset, overwhelmed or distressed. Write this letter from you, to you.

1. List activities that you find comforting.
2. Record the names and phone numbers of supportive friends or family members.
3. Remind yourself of your strengths and virtues.
4. Remind yourself of your special talents, abilities, and interests.
5. Remind yourself of some of your hopes and dreams for the future.
6. Give yourself special advice or other reminders important to you.

You deserve the comfort your Rainy Day Letter will bring. Rereading it and implementing some of the ideas in our letter really can make a difference in times of stress and distress.

Afterward read your letter aloud to the group, or if you prefer, simply describe what it was like to write your letter and how you plan to use it.

AN ANIMAL SYMBOL

If you could be any animal, what would you choose to be? Chances are your choice says something about your Authentic Self.

 One Small Step
Draw a picture of this animal, and then write a description of the animal's special characteristics and habits. What qualities do you find most appealing about this animal?

Now pretend that you are in fact the animal you have selected, and take some time to imagine yourself as this animal. How would you spend a typical day? What do you like and dislike about being this animal?

This exercise will help you discover new alternatives for best expressing your various personality traits. You will also explore how you spend your time.

CHALLENGING THE PROSPERITY MIND-SET

Possibilities
- What things do you associate with a pleasing, prosperous life?
- What aspects of these things are more associated with behavior or personal style than money?
- Which are more dependent on money?
- Can you give yourself some of these things now?
- How might you use your personal creativity to facilitate this? What would be the first small step?

While your list may contain descriptions of things that only additional money could buy, most people also list things that are not dependent on acquiring more money. Once identified, at least some of the things you associate with prosperity may well be within reach.

FIGURING OUT WHO YOU ARE APART FROM YOUR "SHOULDS"

One Small Step
If left unfettered, but nurtured and supported, how would you choose to pass your time? Notice what thoughts and images come to mind as you imagine this.

Possibilities
- If you lived more in accord with your envisioned preferences rather than spending so much time on what you "should" do, what productive or useful things might occur in your life?
- What is one small step you could take to initiate some of these newly discovered activities?
- What small sign would show that you had begun to move in this direction?

Arrange to take this first small step and report the results back to the group.

A SYMBOL FOR THE TIME OF YOUR LIFE

This exercise will help you discover your own unique symbol to remind you to live fully and give priority to the things that really matter to you. Read the instructions completely before doing this exercise so you won't have to interrupt yourself while in the middle of it.

 One Small Step
Find a comfortable place to sit where you will not be disturbed for the next fifteen minutes. Concentrate on your breathing until you achieve a comfortable state and feel centered in your body. Now close your eyes and gently ask your unconscious to give you a symbol that will remind you to spend your time in satisfying and heartfelt ways.

Sit quietly and notice what comes to mind after you ask yourself for a symbol. It may be an image, words, or a feeling. Once you know what it is, write or draw your symbol so you will remember it in the future.

After the group meeting, place your symbol in a place where you will see it often.

PRACTICING DYING

The following exercise will help you shift into your own wise perspective about how to spend the time you still have available in your life. Record your response so that you can refer to it afterward.

 One Small Step
Imagine that you have been told that you have only six months to live. Assume for the purposes of this exercise that although you have an incurable illness, thanks to the miracles of modern medicine you will remain relatively symptom free and able to move around comfortably until the final moments of your life.

 Possibilities
• How would you wish to spend the remaining months of your life?
• Who are the people you would want to spend time with?
• What places would you like to visit or revisit?
• Are there any specific things you would need to do to enhance a feeling of completion and peacefulness before you die?

Take a few moments now to examine your responses to the above questions; they hold valuable clues as to how you might best prioritize your time and more fully honor your most heartfelt longings and needs.

What would be the first small step you could take to incorporate these changes into your daily life? Now embark on this first project in the next week and report the results back to the group.

REWRITING NEGATIVE MESSAGES

 One Small Step
Consider what negative or destructive message from your past interferes with your confidence or your positive feelings about your life. Now think of a new and healthy message you would like to receive instead. Write the new message several times with each hand until it begins to feel like a familiar part of your belief system. Now share this new message with the group and have each group member say it to you while looking at you.

The impact of this new healthy message can be strengthened by writing it repeatedly after the group meeting. Don't worry if the positive message doesn't feel "real" or accurate the first few times you write it or when you hear it from the other group members. As you continue to practice it, it will gradually surface in your behavior and the way you think about yourself and your life.

A RAINY DAY LETTER FROM THE GROUP

When one member is leaving a group, a Rainy Day Letter from the Group is something she can carry away with her after the meeting.

 One Small Step
The person leaving the group starts a letter addressed to herself, Dear (her own name). Then she passes the letter around to the rest of the group. The other group members write messages of comfort and reassurance for the person to whom the letter is addressed. Later she can reread the letter to reconnect to the feelings of support and validation she received from the group.

When a group is coming to a close, a Rainy Day Letter is something each member can take away after their last meeting.

 One Small Step
Each group member starts a letter addressed to them, Dear (their own name). All the letters are passed around to each of the other members of the group. Group members write messages of comfort and reassurance for the person to whom the letter is addressed. Later each person can reread her letter to reconnect to the feelings of support and validation she received from the group.

A Rainy Day Letter from the Group is a good way to end a Small Steps Support Group or to provide support and closure when someone is leaving the group.

SUGGESTED READING LIST

Bender, Sue. *Everyday Sacred: A Woman's Journey Home*. San Francisco: HarperSan Francisco, 1995.

Berg, Insoo Kim and Scott D. Miller. *The Miracle Method: A Radically New Approach to Problem Drinking*. New York: W. W. Norton, 1995.

Bolen, Jean Shinoda. *Crossing to Avalon: A Woman's Midlife Pilgrimage*. San Francisco: HarperSan Francisco, 1994.

Breathnach, Sarah Ban. *Simple Abundance: A Daybook of Comfort and Joy*. New York: Warner, 1995.

Cameron, Julia. *The Artist's Way: A Spiritual Path to Higher Creativity*. New York: Tarcher, 1992.

Capacchione, Lucia. *The Creative Journal: The Art of Finding Yourself*. Athens, Ohio: Swallow Press Books, 1979.

Csikszentmihalyi, Mihaly. *Flow: The Psychology of Optimal Experience*. New York: HarperCollins, 1990.

de Shazer, Steve. *Keys to Solution in Brief Therapy*. New York: W. W. Norton, 1985.

—. *Putting Difference to Work*. New York: W. W. Norton, 1991.

Estes, Clarissa Pinkola *Women Who Run With the Wolves: Myths and Stories of the Wild Woman Archetype*. New York: Ballantine, 1992.

Field, Joanna. *A Life of One's Own*. New York: Tarcher, 1981.

Freedman, Jill and Gene Combs. *Narrative Therapy: Social Construction of Preferred Realities*. New York: W. W. Norton, 1996.

Gawain, Shakti. *Creative Visualization*. New York: Bantam, 1983.

Gilligan, Stephen. *The Courage to Love: Principles and Practices of Self-Relations Psychotherapy*. New York: W. W. Norton, 1997.

Holzer, Burghild Nina. *A Walk Between Heaven and Earth: A Personal Journal on Writing the Creative Process*. New York. Bell Tower, 1994.

Lindbergh, Anne Morrow. *Gift from the Sea*. New York: Vintage, 1978.

Livingstone, Angela. *Salome: Her Life and Work*. London: Gordon Fraser, 1984.

Louden, Jennifer. *The Woman's Comfort Book: A Self-Nurturing Guide for Restoring Balance in Your Life*. San Francisco: HarperSan Francisco, 1992.

Martz, Sandra Haldeman. *If I Had My Life To Live Over I Would Pick More Daisies*. Watsonville, CA: Papier-Mache Press, 1992.

Metzger, Deena. *Writing for Your Life: A Guide and Companion to the Inner Worlds*. San Francisco: Harper, 1992.

Suggested Reading List

Mitchell, Stephen, ed. *The Enlightened Mind An Anthology of Sacred Prose* New York: HarperPerennial, 1993.

Napier, Nancy. *Sacred Practices for Conscious Living* New York: W. W. Norton, 1997

Peck, M. Scott. *The Road Less Traveled and Beyond Spiritual Growth in an Age of Anxiety* New York: Simon & Schuster, 1977.

Rechtschaffen, Stephan. *Time Shifting: Creating More Time to Enjoy Your Life.* New York: Doubleday, 1996.

Rossi, Ernest L. *Twenty-Minute Break: Reduce Stress, Maximize Performance, and Improve Health and Emotional Well-Being Using the New Science of Ultradian Rhythms* Los Angeles: Tarcher, 1991.

Rossi, Ernest L. and Katherine Lane Rossi, eds. *The Symptom Path to Enlightenment The New Dynamics of Self-Organization in Hypnotherapy, An Advanced Manual for Beginners* Pacific Palisades, CA: Gateway, 1996.

Schiller, David. *The Little Zen Companion* New York: Workman, 1994.

Schnarch, David. *Passionate Marriage: Love, Sex, and Intimacy in Emotionally Committed Relationships.* New York: W. W. Norton, 1997.

Shaughnessy, Susan. *Walking on Alligators A Book of Meditations for Writers* San Francisco: Harper, 1993.

St. James, Elaine. *Inner Simplicity 100 Ways to Regain Peace and Nourish Your Soul* New York: Hyperion, 1995.

Walters, Catherine and Ronald Havens. *Hypnotherapy for Health, Harmony, and Peak Performance Expanding the Goals of Hypnotherapy* New York: Brunner/Mazel, 1993.

Weiner-Davis, Michele. *Divorce Busting: A Revolutionary and Rapid Program for Staying Together,* New York. Summit, 1992.

Wolinsky, Stephen. *Hearts on Fire The Tao of Meditation* San Diego: Blue Dove Press, 1996.

—-. *Trances People Live: Healing Approaches in Quantum Psychology* Norfolk, CT: Bramble, 1991.

Wolinsky, Stephen and Kristi Kennen. *Quantum Consciousness. The Guide to Experiencing Quantum Psychology* Norfolk, CT: Bramble, 1993

BIBLIOGRAPHY

Bell-Gadsby, Cheryl and Ann Siegenberg. *Reclaiming Herstory: Ericksonian Solution-Focused Therapy for Sexual Abuse* New York: Brunner/Mazel, 1995.

Bender, Sue. *Everyday Sacred· A Woman's Journey Home.* New York: HarperCollins, 1995.

Berg, Insoo Kim. *So What Else Is Better? Solutions for Substance Abuse.* Videotape. Milwaukee, WI: Brief Family Therapy Center, 1995.

—-. *A Solution-Focused Approach to Family Based Services* Milwaukee, WI: Brief Family Therapy Center Publications, 1990.

Berg, Insoo Kim and Scott D. Miller. *Working with the Problem Drinker: A Solution-Focused Approach.* New York: W. W. Norton, 1992.

Berg, Insoo Kim and Steve de Shazer. "Making Numbers Talk: Language in Therapy." In *The New Language of Change· Constructive Collaboration in Psychotherapy,* edited by Steven Friedman, 5-24. New York: Guilford, 1993.

Bolen, Jean Shinoda. *Crossing to Avalon· A Woman's Midlife Pilgrimage.* San Francisco: HarperSan Francisco, 1994.

Breathnach, Sarah Ban *Simple Abundance: A Daybook of Comfort and Joy.* New York: Warner, 1995.

Bristol, Claude M. *The Magic of Believing: The Science of Setting Your Goal and Then Reaching It.* New York: Simon & Schuster, 1948.

Cameron, Julia. *The Artist's Way A Spiritual Path to Higher Creativity.* New York: Tarcher, 1992.

Capacchione, Lucia. *The Creative Journal The Art of Finding Yourself.* Athens, Ohio: Swallow Press Books, 1979.

Castaneda, Carlos. *The Teachings of Don Juan: A Yaqui Way of Knowledge.* Berkeley: U.C. Press, 1968.

Crowley, Ronald and Joyce Mills. *Therapeutic Metaphors for Children and the Child Within.* New York: Brunner/Mazel, 1986.

Csikszentmihalyi, Mihaly. *Flow· The Psychology of Optimal Experience* New York: HarperCollins, 1990.

de Shazer, Steve. *Patterns of Brief Family Therapy· An Ecosystem Approach.* New York: Guilford, 1982.

—-. *Clues: Investigating Solutions in Brief Therapy* New York: W. W. Norton, 1988.

—-. *Keys to Solution in Brief Therapy* New York: W. W. Norton, 1985.

—-."Only Once If I Really Mean It: Brief Treatment of a Previously Dissociated Incest Case." *Journal of Strategic and Systemic Therapies,* Vol. 8, 4 (1989): 3-8.

—-. *A Path with a Heart Ericksonian Utilization with Resistant and Chronic Clients.* New York: Brunner/Mazel, 1985.

——. *Putting Difference to Work* New York: W. W. Norton, 1991.

——. *Resolving Sexual Abuse. Solution-Focused Therapy and Ericksonian Hypnosis for Adult Survivors.* New York: W. W. Norton, 1991.

——. "Solution-Focused Therapy with a Case of Severe Abuse." In *Constructive Therapies*, edited by Michael F. Hoyt, 276-294. New York: Guilford, 1994a.

——. *Words Were Originally Magic* New York: W. W. Norton, 1994.

de Shazer, Steve, Insoo Kim Berg, Eve Lipchik, Elan Nunally, Alex Molnar, Wallace Gingerich, and Michele Weiner-Davis. "Brief Therapy: Focused Solution Development." *Family Process* 25 (1986): 207-222.

Dolan, Yvonne. "An Ericksonian Perspective on the Treatment of Sexual Abuse." In *Ericksonian Methods. The Essence of the Story*, edited by Jeffrey K. Zeig, 395-414. New York: Guilford, 1994b.

Erickson, Milton H. "Further Techniques of Hypnosis: Utilization Techniques." *American Journal of Clinical Hypnosis*, 2, (1959): 3-21.

——. "Naturalistic Techniques of Hypnosis: Utilization Techniques." *American Journal of Clinical Hypnosis*, 1, (1958): 3-8.

——. "The Use of Symptoms As an Integral Part of Therapy." *American Journal of Clinical Hypnosis*, 8, (1965): 198-209.

Erickson, Milton H., Ernest L. Rossi, and Sheila K. Rossi. *Hypnotic Realities* New York: Irvington, 1976.

Estes, Clarissa Pinkola. *Women Who Run With the Wolves: Myths and Stories of the Wild Woman Archetype* New York: Ballantine, 1992.

Field, Joanna. *A Life of One's Own.* New York: Tarcher, 1981.

Furman, Ben and Tapani Ahola. *Solution Talk. Hosting the Therapeutic Conversations* New York: W. W. Norton, 1992.

——. "Solution Talk: The Solution-Oriented Way of Talking about Problems." In *Constructive Therapies*, edited by Michael F. Hoyt, 41-66. New York: Guilford, 1994.

Haley, Jay and Madeline Richeport. *Milton H Erickson, MD. Explorer in Hypnosis and Therapy.* Rockville, MD: Triangle Productions Videotape, 1993.

Holzer, Burghild Nina. *A Walk Between Heaven and Earth. A Personal Journal on Writing and the Creative Process.* New York: Bell Tower, 1994.

Jung, Carl Gustav. *Memories, Dreams, Reflections* New York: Vintage, 1965.

Kerr, Michael and Murray Bowen. *Family Evaluation. An Approach Based on Bowen Theory* New York: W. W. Norton, 1988.

Bibliography

Lipchik, Eve. "Purposeful Sequences for Beginning the Solution-Focused Interview." In *Interviewing*, edited by Eve Lipchik, 105-117. Rockville, MD: Aspen, 1988.

Lipchik, Eve and Steve de Shazer. "The Purposeful Interview." *Journal of Strategic and Systemic Therapies* Vol. 5, 1-2 (1986): 88-89.

Livingstone, Angela. *Salome: Her Life and Works*. London: Gordon Fraser, 1984.

Louden, Jennifer. *The Woman's Comfort Book: A Self-Nurturing Guide for Restoring Balance in Your Life*. San Francisco: HarperSan Francisco, 1992.

Love Quotations from the Heart. Philadelphia: Running Press Book Publishers, 1990.

Metzger, Deena. *Writing for Your Life: A Guide and Companion to the Inner Worlds*. San Francisco: Harper, 1992.

Mitchell, Stephen. *The Gospel According to Jesus: A New Translation Guide to His Essential Teachings for Believers and Unbelievers* New York: HarperCollins, 1993.

—, ed. *The Enlightened Mind· An Anthology of Sacred Prose* New York: HarperPerennial, 1993.

Neruda, Pablo. English translation by Kenneth Krabbenhoft, *Odes to Opposites*. New York: Little, Brown, & Co., 1994.

Ogden, Nash. *I'm a Stranger Here Myself*. Boston: Little, Brown and Company, 1938.

O'Hanlon, Bill and Michele Weiner-Davis. *In Search of Solutions*. New York: W. W. Norton, 1989.

Parker, Dorothy W. *The Poetry and Short Stories of Dorothy Parker*. New York: Random House, 1994.

Rechtschaffen, Stephan. *Time Shifting: Creating More Time to Enjoy Your Life*. New York: Doubleday, 1996.

Redman, Alvin, ed. *The Wit and Humor of Oscar Wilde*. New York: Dover, 1959.

Rossi, Ernest L. *Twenty-Minute Break: Reduce Stress, Maximize Performance, and Improve Health and Emotional Well-Being Using the New Science of Ultradian Rhythms*. Los Angeles: Tarcher, 1991.

—, ed. *The Collected Papers of Milton Erickson, Vol. I*. New York: Irvington, 1980.

Saine, Thomas P. and Jeffrey L. Sammons, eds. *Goethe, The Collected Works, Vol. 4*. Princeton, New Jersey: Princeton University Press, 1987.

Sarton, May. *Journal of a Solitude*. New York: W. W. Norton, 1973.

Schiller, David. *The Little Zen Companion*. New York: Workman, 1994.

Schnarch, David. *Passionate Marriage: Love, Sex, and Intimacy in Emotionally Committed Relationships*. New York: W. W. Norton, 1997.

Shaughnessy, Susan. *Walking on Alligators: A Book of Meditations for Writers*. San Francisco: Harper, 1993.

St. James, Elaine. *Inner Simplicity: 100 Ways to Regain Peace and Nourish Your Soul*. New York: Hyperion, 1995.

Bibliography

Synder, Mark and Phyllis White. "Moods, Memories: Elation, Depression, and the Remembering of the Events of One's Life." *Journal of Personality,* 50, 2 (1982): 149-167.

Too, Lillian. *The Complete Illustrated Guide to Feng Shui. How to Apply the Secrets of Chinese Wisdom for Health, Wealth and Happiness* London: Element Publishers, 1996.

Walters, Catherine and Ronald Havens. *Hypnotherapy for Health, Harmony, and Peak Performance. Expanding the Goals of Hypnotherapy.* New York: Brunner/Mazel, 1993.

Wapnick, Kenneth. From a talk given on A Course in Miracles. Roscoe, New York: Foundation for A Course in Miracles, 1983.

Weiner-Davis, Michele. *Divorce Busting: A Revolutionary and Rapid Program for Staying Together* New York: Summit, 1992.

Weiner-Davis, Michele, Steve de Shazer, and Wallace Gingerich. "Building on Pretreatment Change to Construct the Therapeutic Solution: An Exploratory Study." *Journal of Marital and Family Therapy,* Vol. 13, 4, (1987): 359-363.

Wells, Rebecca. *Divine Secrets of the Ya-Ya Sisterhood.* New York: HarperCollins, 1996.

Wolinsky, Stephen. *Hearts on Fire: The Tao of Meditation* San Diego: Blue Dove Press, 1996.

Important Notes to Yourself

IMPORTANT NOTES TO YOURSELF

IMPORTANT NOTES TO YOURSELF

Important Notes to Yourself

IMPORTANT NOTES TO YOURSELF

IMPORTANT NOTES TO YOURSELF

ABOUT THE AUTHOR

YVONNE DOLAN, MA, has been a psychotherapist for twenty-three years. She first worked with traumatized patients at a shelter for teenage runaways in New Orleans in the early 1980s and has specialized since that time in helping people overcome the effects of abuse and other traumatic experiences. Recognized as an expert in her field, she has been interviewed on television and radio about treating trauma and abuse.

In addition to her private practice, Yvonne conducts training seminars on Solution-focused therapy and Ericksonian hypnotherapy throughout the U.S., Canada, and Europe and in Australia, Japan, Korea, and South America for psychotherapists and other health care professionals. She also teaches workshops for the public.

Yvonne's two previous books are *Resolving Sexual Abuse* (W.W. Norton, 1991) and *A Path with a Heart* (Brunner/Mazel, 1985). She has also published numerous articles and chapters in psychotherapy publications and journals.

Yvonne lives with her husband, Charlie Johnson, in the foothills of the Colorado Rocky Mountains where she pits her gardening skills against the appetites of a large herd of wild elk and a group of small but voracious rabbits.